854583

THE INVASION BEFORE NORMANDY

Also by Edwin P. Hoyt:

U-Boat Wars
Defeat at the Falklands
The Kamikazes

THE INVASION BEFORE NORMANDY

The Secret Battle of Slapton Sands

EDWIN P. HOYT

ROBERT HALE · LONDON

First published in Great Britain 1987

Robert Hale Limited
Clerkenwell House
Clerkenwell Green
London EC1R 0HT

British Library Cataloguing in Publication Data
Hoyt, Edwin P.
   The Invasion before Normandy: the secret
   battle of Slapton Sands.
   1. World War, 1939–1945—Campaigns—
   France—Normandy   2. World War, 1939–1945
   —Naval operations
   I. Title
   940.54'21   D75.6.N6
   ISBN 0-7090-2598-X

Printed in Great Britain by
St Edmundsbury Press Limited, Bury St Edmunds, Suffolk
and bound by WBC Bookbinders Limited

CONTENTS

To the memory of those who died at Slapton Sands.
Their sacrifice was not in vain.

INTRODUCTION

Early in 1984, nearly forty years after the end of World War II, a strange and nasty rumor coursed across the fields and beaches of the southwest English countryside. It hinted of dark doings by high authority in the penultimate year of the war, as the Western Allies were preparing to invade Adolf Hitler's Fortress Europe.

Several hundred bodies of American soldiers were said to be buried in a huge, unmarked grave in a pasture on a Devon farm owned by Nolan Tope. Curiosity seekers began coming to the farm to poke about, although they were not welcomed by the owner. Mr. Tope scoffed at the rumors and indicated he would prefer not to have unwanted visitors wandering about his farm during spring lambing.

The story, fired by some longtime residents of the area who claimed knowledge of at least part of the dreadful secret, would not die down. Dorothy Seekings was the most outspoken resident. In the spring of 1944, said Ms. Seekings, when she was twenty-three years old, she had seen the bodies. She knew they were Americans because they wore American uniforms.

There had been strange doings in Devon during that winter of 1944. The whole section around the South Hams area where the farm is located had been taken over by the American military. Some three thousand residents of farms and villages had been ejected from their homes, promised compensation for damages, and told to go away and keep silent. It was a tribute to the English character that virtually no one objected loudly.

"It was a question of doing your bit for the war effort," said John Hannaford, a butcher at Torcross who was seventeen in 1944. "We were told to get out and it was a year before we were allowed to return."

Ms. Seekings was a rare exception, and only because her father was a baker,

11

and the American troops in the training establishments in the Dartmouth area needed his services, and he, in turn, needed his daughter's help to deliver the baked goods.

The American bodies, said Ms. Seekings, had been laid out on the ground like rows of cordwood—while bulldozers dug the mass grave. Ms. Seekings was cautioned at the time never to mention what she had seen. For forty years, not knowing quite what her secret was, she kept it. But in the spring of 1984, when England and France prepared to celebrate with lavish ceremonial the 40th anniversary of the beginning of the liberation of Europe from Hitler's Nazi occupation, her story came out.

"The bodies were in American uniforms," she told a British newspaperman who was poking around among the rumors. "There were great mounds of earth in the field and I was told they were going to be buried there. I certainly never heard that they were moved."

Who were these hundreds of American dead, so dishonored by their own countrymen that they were buried in a mass grave, and the manner of their deaths concealed from the world by military secrecy?

Was there any truth to the story?

What Ms. Seekings said, had been true at a point. Several years ago, while beginning research for a book on World War II, I had letters from several participants in the D-Day activities which referred to mysterious doings on the Devon coast in the spring of 1944.

David A. Roop, in 1944 Lieutenant Roop, chief engineer of *LST 515,* wrote me:

> There was a naval engagement in the English Channel that cost the lives of approximately 750 American soldiers and sailors. I have never read of this engagement nor heard of any acknowledgment by the United States government that it ever happened.
>
> I was there. It was between . . . LSTs . . . and an unknown number of German E-Boats. All ships were loaded with army troops, equipment, vehicles and tanks.
>
> If the ship's log of the LST 515 from April 25, 1944 to May 3, 1944 were perused, you sir, would have a scoop.
>
> I firmly believe that the 750 who died were lumped into the casualties suffered at Normandy.

Actually, Mr. Roop's contention was a little off on the facts, although, since he relied on sheer memory, that is not surprising. A few references to the events of late April 1944 are to be found in books about the invasion of France. The official U.S. Army history volume, *Cross Channel Attack,* by G. A. Harrison, mentions the happenings, without, however, a great deal of detail, or any mention of the mass burial, For my purposes at the time, the story was one of those odd little sidelights of history which seem interesting, but hardly worth exploring for their own sakes, more properly the province of a daily newspaper, magazine, or television report than the subject of a book.

And that is what happened.

A *New York Times* reporter named Jon Nordheimer heard the tale of the Devon coast and began to do some investigating. He consulted American military records at the U.S. National Archives and Carlisle Barracks and learned the secret of the mystery. The 750 Americans—749, in fact—were victims of an attack by German motor torpedo boats on an American convoy bringing troops to the South Devon coast to participate in one of the last exercises of the Allied forces prior to the invasion of Normandy on June 6, 1944.

It all began with Winston Churchill during the darkest times of the war against Hitler, when he foresaw that one day the Allies would invade Fortress Europe and therefore secured a commitment from President Franklin D. Roosevelt to place the European war on the American agenda ahead of the war against Japan. In 1942 the Allies began the planning that led to this disaster off the south Devon coast. The exercise that was interrupted by German submarines was a rehearsal for the landings on Utah beach at the base of the Cotentin Peninsula of Normandy that would occur six weeks later.

Here is the story of what happened.

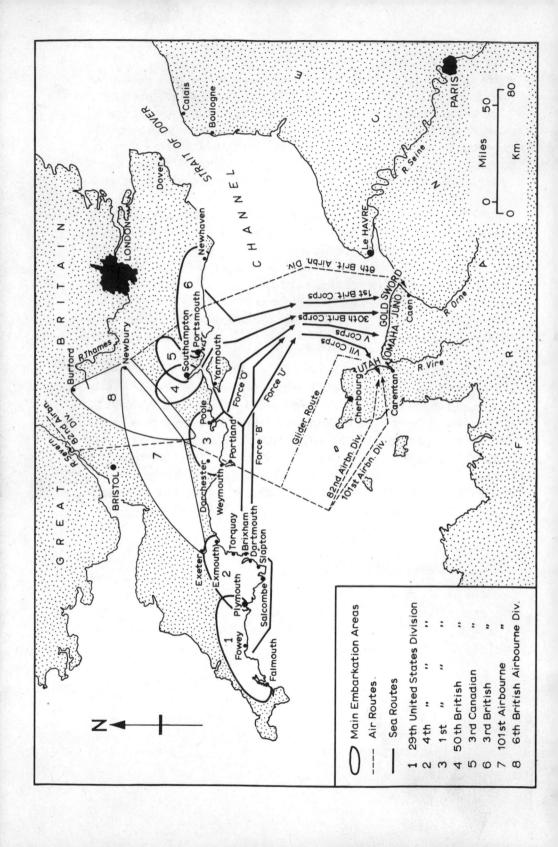

1

Planning

WINSTON CHURCHILL was the progenitor. In the dismal days of 1941 when Britain was battling for survival, largely alone, the Americans as yet not totally committed, and the commonwealth unable to give the volume of support that could bring victory, Churchill still reserved a corner of his mind for consideration of that day when a decisive assault could be made against German-occupied Europe. To be sure, the British prime minister was not the most avid advocate of the cross-channel attack, but he did get everyone else thinking. His grand design called for forty armored divisions and a million other troops to land in Europe in 1943.

By the spring of 1942 Churchill's prodding (and Stalin's nagging for a second front) had elicited from the American Joint Chiefs of Staff a plan for the use of forty-eight divisions. The attack was to be made across the English Channel. The strike force was to hit on selected beaches between Le Havre and Boulogne, initially using six divisions, supported by airborne troops. Harry Hopkins called it "a frontal assault upon the enemy in northern France in 1943," and the Americans even had a name for it: Operation Roundup.

For the next two years Churchill continued to believe that the assault should be made on what he called "the soft underbelly of Europe," the Balkans, or that it should be diffused to many areas, thus giving the Germans more than they could handle anywhere. But this view received no American support, and British objections to the hammerlike cross-channel thrust were met by American belief that the British were still suffering from the trench warfare syndrome of World War I, during which the cream of Britain's (and France's) youth had been decimated in hammer attacks against a powerful foe.

Churchill was careful never to close a door, no matter his own beliefs. "... I had to work by influence and diplomacy in order to secure agreed and harmonious action with our cherished ally, without whose aid nothing but ruin faced the world . . ."

The planning began. By the summer of 1942, Churchill saw that preparations for the cross-channel attack had to be separated from operations. In June Harry Hopkins introduced Churchill to General Dwight D. Eisenhower and General Mark Clark, and they spent an hour discussing the cross-channel attack. Churchill was shrewd enough to recognize that the meeting had a special significance. Gradually he was abandoning his countersuggestions for feints and lesser attacks elsewhere. Also, by July 1942, it seemed doubtful if an assault across the English Channel could be mounted in 1943, and the words "or later" had begun to be heard in inter-Allied conversations.

Churchill had always fancied his own code names for military and naval operations. He detested "Roundup," partly because it was a pure Americanism, "this boastful, ill-chosen name." Quietly he made his own plans. It was assumed throughout England that a Briton would be in charge of the invasion.

The Americans had no such assumption. On the contrary, President Roosevelt knew very well that American public opinion would not countenance the employment of a major U.S. force under a foreign commander. Most of the British did not recognize that reality, nor did they understand that most Americans were far more concerned with the war against Japan than with the one against Germany. For until the U-boat campaign of 1942 the Germans had really never done anything to the United States, and as the plans for the invasion of Europe were begun, the full effect of that German foray on the sea had not yet been totally appreciated in America.

Clearly the attitudes of the Americans presented a difficulty for the British. Soon the question had to be brought into the open: who was to lead this cross-channel attack, an American or a Briton?

The British believed it should be one of their own because they, after all, had the experience in fighting the Germans. Up to and after the Casablanca Conference, the British believed the Americans would take a secondary role, supplying the force, but letting the British lead. Politically speaking, however, it was apparent from the beginning that if the cross-channel attack was to have major American support, the overall commander had to be an American—a fact Churchill soon appreciated. Churchill never lost sight of the politics of the war, nor of the innate anti-British feelings of many Americans. Because of his enlightened self-interest as well as his personal leanings, Britain could count on President Franklin Roosevelt. But Roosevelt, as Churchill knew, had a constituency that had to be considered. The American military men could not take a back seat, even if they had been willing to do so.

There came the first rub. The British military had very little respect for the

American army. On a trip to America in June 1942, Churchill and Major General Sir Hastings Ismay, the prime minister's chief of staff and deputy secretary to the War Cabinet, visited South Carolina to observe American armor, infantry, and airborne troops in maneuvers. "To put these troops against continental troops would be murder," said General Ismay. The chief of staff's observation about the quality of the American soldier was representative of the British military and extended all the way up the ladder. The only American general the British really respected was George C. Marshall. Churchill suggested his name as commander of the combined operation that would attack Fortress Europe. President Roosevelt indicated his general approval, but no decision was made. It was always Roosevelt's way to avoid a difficult decision until the last, and besides, by November 1942 it was apparent to British and Americans that the 1943 date for the cross-channel attack was going to be impossible. The resources could not be pulled together and moved across the Atlantic that quickly. The year 1943 would have to be a year of lesser operations, while the planning and the supply problems of the major invasion were resolved.

Once it was mutually recognized that the cross-channel attack was even further away than had been expected, in order to keep the Germans off balance and placate Stalin, several lesser operations were carried out late in 1942 and in 1943: the invasions of North Africa, Sicily, and Italy. To the Americans, there was never any question but that these were sideshows. The buildup of divisions, air power, and naval power for the cross-channel attack continued in England.

Before that, however, by mid-November 1942, the planning of the European war had reached a crisis stage, "a sort of combined deadlock," Churchill called it. The British feared that the Americans were leaning toward abandoning the European theater and concentrating their efforts against Japan. Harry Hopkins had told Churchill that the war against Japan had captured the American public fancy far more securely than the war against the Germans. President Roosevelt felt constrained to reassure Churchill that "we of course have no intention of abandoning 'Roundup.'"

By January 1943, Churchill had won a point: the name of the cross-channel attack was changed from Operation Roundup to Operation Overlord. The target date was moved to the first half of 1944. At the Casablanca Conference in January 1943, the British and the Americans agreed to establish a combined staff to prepare a definitive plan for the invasion. It was agreed that the overall commander would be an American, but the Americans were not ready to name anyone. The unknown's chief of staff would have to be

British. He would be known as COSSAC—"Chief of Staff, Supreme Allied Commander (designate)."

The British already had a good deal of experience in such planning, most of it coming to nought, under the Combined Operations Headquarters established early in the war to think out such operations as the Dieppe raid. These were the commandos, and the chief of the headquarters was Vice Admiral Lord Louis Mountbatten. But Mountbatten was much too highly placed to do for this sort of job, and needed was a less definitely British establishment type, someone who had shown an ability to get along with Americans. Chosen tentatively was Lieutenant General Frederick Morgan, newly appointed commander of the British I Corps, who was then scheduled for the North Africa theater of General Eisenhower. Morgan had one other attribute: he firmly believed in the cross-channel attack, unlike many of the British generals, who instinctively recoiled from "the butcher's bill" of a frontal assault against the Germans.

On March 12, 1943, Morgan was told to report to General Ismay. He was instructed to produce a master plan, virtually overnight, for the organization of a staff. On his second attempt he came up with something the British chiefs of staff could accept as a beginning. Morgan was invited to lunch at Chequers, the country estate of the prime minister, and there it was decided that he "would do."

From the outset, mounting a joint operation was a Herculean task. Consider one small point: the difference (.003 caliber) between British and American rifles. Were the Americans, or the British, to retool? The answer was neither. The British and American forces would be kept severely apart at the operational level. The British would fight with British and the Americans with Americans. But they would fight together, against a common enemy. That was the thrust of the cross-channel attack planning from the outset.

General Morgan became COSSAC. He immediately appointed an American, Brigadier General Ray W. Barker, as his deputy. Staff officers were British and American; navy, army, and air force officers each had his Allied counterpart. Administration was joint. Only the responsibility for intelligence was handed over to the British because of their network of agents across the channel and their four years' experience in the field.

COSSAC was to plan for three immediate tasks:

The first plan was to pin down the German forces in Western Europe so they could not move east against the Russians. This was a direct result of Stalin's demand for a second front, a demand that the Western Allies were not prepared to meet in 1943.

The second plan was a contingency plan for a hasty return to the European continent if the German armies suddenly disintegrated under the weight of so many blows struck from so many directions.

The third plan was the most important, the COSSAC plan for a full-scale assault against Fortress Europe. The date was now changed, and an assault as early as possible in 1944 was to be prepared.

These requirements were thrust upon General Morgan almost casually, one day in March 1943. Then came the snapper: the British chiefs of staff, who were taking the responsibility for this initial phase of planning, wanted immediate results. General Morgan was instructed to have his three plans ready by early July.

Morgan set to work. He was given the task of preparing the way for an unknown commander, and he had not been told that it was going to be an American.

From the outset the combined staff had to operate within the framework of British-American distrust, a factor discussed fully by General Morgan in his memoirs. The approach of Briton and American to nearly every military problem was different. For instance, in the Battle of Britain, the British had been well served by their Spitfire fighters. One of the Spitfire fighter's basic qualities was short range, the range sacrificed in favor of speed. That quality was a negative for operations into the heart of Germany. The Americans wanted long-range fighters, to protect heavy bombers on daylight bombing missions. The British leaned on their experience: night bombing was the way.

It was one of hundreds of major and minor differences of opinion, and bit by bit, these disagreements had to be overcome. General Morgan:

"There were incessant clashes of personality, and these, moreover, occurred not only between nation and nation or between service and service. It is no use denying that there are Americans who cannot take British just as there are British who cannot take Americans. At the same time there were cases on the COSSAC staff of British officers who inspired the admiration and affection of their American colleagues, but who lacked the power to collaborate with their own British comrades, and vice versa. . . . There was little time for argument or for the negotiation of personal reconciliations. It was necessary to resort to surgery rather than to medicine."

That spring of 1943, the staff of the still unchosen Supreme Allied Commander set up shop in Norfolk House on St. James's Square in London, a place appropriate for two reasons: it was the birthplace of King George III, the last ruler of both England and America, and as the former offices of any number of "planners," it was the homesite of so many unfulfilled and sometimes ridiculous plans that the military public tended to regard anything that came out of Norfolk House as a joke. So, hopefully, would enemy agents. General Morgan and his staff connived to secure a mess, or club, for the staff members, including dining facilities and a bar. In wartime London this was virtually a miracle.

Given the amenities, the staff of the supreme commander set to work to plan an offensive into the heart of the enemy's country. Actually the planners had to work in three directions at once: first, to plan a diversionary operation, to fool the Germans, second, to plan a pick-up-the-pieces operation, or several of them, to take advantage of German collapses in one area or another, and third, to plan for that major assault across the channel.

The whole was seriously endangered from time to time by eruptions from within the British establishment, calling for major operations in the Mediterranean. Prime Minister Churchill wielded his famous red pen one time to produce a memo outlining an attack in the Mediterranean involving the whole of British and American might. This memo upset the Americans more than a little. And on the British side, there was a basic distrust of American intentions; the British did not want to set up a trans-channel operation and then be left by their allies holding the bag.

As for the first plan, diversion, from the beginning it was given enormous emphasis by the British, somewhat to the surprise of the Americans. But the problem of forces indicates why it was essential that the Germans be fooled from the beginning. In 1943 the Americans had only a single combat division in England. In the early months of 1943, the British had to depend on their own resources to try to fool the Germans into believing the invasion was coming in one area. The area chosen was the Pas de Calais region, the shortest passage across the English Channel from England to France. It was the logical point of invasion, just as it had been the jumping-off point the Germans had proposed to use in their 1940 preparations to capture the British Isles.

The media were encouraged to speculate on the invasion site, and at least one magazine hit on the right solution, but this was genially ignored along with all the other journalistic ventures into military planning that put the invasion in Norway, along the Dutch coast, on the Cotentin peninsula, or elsewhere. One beauty of this sort of war was that the authorities did not have to *do* anything to save the day. The important matter was to keep the Germans off guard. COSSAC concentrated its efforts on making everything look as though a troop and supply buildup was being made in southeast England, whereas the real concentrations had to be made in southwest England. A program of improving roads and airfields in the southeast was begun to fool the Germans.

General Morgan and his staff had one thing going for them: the logical German mind. OKW, the German general staff, believed that since this area was the shortest distance between the two warring regions, it should logically be the focal point of attack. Why should the Allies consider going west to Normandy and then having to double back toward Paris and Berlin? Why indeed? The Germans had planned their invasion of Britain from the Pas de Calais toward the southern counties. Was it not obvious that the British would do the same in reverse to save materiel, men, and time?

So, as many landing craft as could be spared from actual operations and training (and it was not a great number) were brought around to southeastern England. Where more were needed, the camouflage experts constructed fakes, called *bigbobs* and *wetbobs*, which from the air seemed very real, down to the detail of laundry drying on the halyards and smoke drifting from the smokestacks.

The first allied deception operation was called Operation Starkey and was aimed at convincing the Germans that the invasion, when it arrived, would be concentrated against the Pas de Calais. It was to include a feigned amphibious landing called Operation Harlequin.

The Royal Air Force and the U.S. Eighth Air Force were dragooned into planning a major "air battle." Early in August 1943 the increase of activity in southern England brought about an increase in Luftwaffe reconnaissance and bombing along the south coast. The Germans, it seemed, were taking the bait. But the weather turned bad, and British Bomber Command refused to divert as much effort to this game as the COSSAC planners wanted. The navy had been called upon to send several warships to bombard the German-held coast across the channel, but the admirals refused to risk their ships for a ploy. Still, the amphibious game was played out on September 8, 1943; the minesweepers swept channels virtually in the mouths of the German coastal batteries on the French side of the channel. Up the channel after them came an armada of merchant ships and naval vessels, carrying thousands of troops. Operation Harlequin was the army aspect of the game. Overhead flew flocks of fighter and bomber planes, and onto the beaches came the infantry—many of whom had really believed that Operation Harlequin was going to be an invasion across the water. It was not, and the Germans did not seem to rise to the bait. The end of it, it appeared, was a dull thud. The press, which had been quietly encouraged to exercise its right of speculation, had built up the whole operation as the real invasion, and when it turned out to be just an exercise they were indignant. In that sense, Operation Starkey was less than an unmitigated success. But it did have important positive results that were not immediately seen. One, was the realization by many high-ranking British and American officers who observed the operation that the logistical difficulties that would arise in an invasion were far more complex than anyone had recognized. (If a general commanding invasion forces needed an armored division badly, but the line of advance called for delivery of an infantry division, the Operation Starkey plan had no provision for the sort of flexibility that was needed.)

Second, and even more important as it was to turn out, was the conclusion, etched into the German military mind, that the Pas de Calais was indeed scheduled to become the target for the invading Allies. The German Ober-kommandwehrmacht (OKW) were not fooled into believing that Operation Starkey was any more than an exercise, but that did not prevent them from believing that when exercise became invasion, the drill would be much the same, although on an accelerated level. That belief, which the Allies did not fully realize they had succeeded in reinforcing, would turn out to be very important indeed in the first month after June 6, 1944.

In the summer of 1943, Operation Starkey took an enormous amount of the energy of General Morgan and his staff, but their most important task was the creation, virtually from thin air, of a workable plan for the invasion of Hitler's Festung Europa. One of the very real difficulties was that old psychological bugaboo of the British military establishment, as mentioned earlier, the fear of bogging down in trench warfare, or worse, of being trapped at the water's edge. The British did not have to go back to 1915 for that second possibility, the difficulties of Dunkirk and the St. Nazaire and Dieppe raids had brought nightmares to enough minds.

The first raid, St. Nazaire, had been carried out in April 1942. The raid had involved an attack on the port and lock facilities at this important French port. The old U.S. destroyer *Campbeltown* (turned over to the British in the early stages of the American aid program) was intentionally run aground and jammed into the locks. The raiding party then made its escape. There was one apparent failure: the three tons of explosive in the bows of the destroyer did not explode. The next day, however, after hundreds of Germans had come aboard to inspect the vessel, the explosive charge went off creating carnage and knocking out the lock for the rest of the war. It was a successful raid but also a reminder always to expect the unexpected.

The second lesson of 1942 was from the Dieppe raid.

Dieppe is a small port on the English Channel, in the district of Seine Maritime, about halfway between Le Havre and Boulogne, definitely on the Pas de Calais side of the channel. In the spring of 1942 the British chiefs of staff were looking for a spot to launch a raid, partly to keep the Germans off balance, partly to learn about some of the difficulties involved in putting a force ashore in Fortress Europe. Dieppe appealed because intelligence reports indicated it was garrisoned by only a single battalion of second-rate troops and service troops, about 1,400 men in all. On July 3 the Allied troops, mostly Canadians, embarked from the Isle of Wight for Dieppe, but bad weather postponed the attack for four days. German aircraft found the raiders' vessels and attacked. The landing was called off, and the troops disembarked from their ships. General Bernard Montgomery, who was then commander of the Southeastern Command and thus in charge of the operation, tried to get it canceled because he feared that security had been completely compromised, and the element of surprise was going to be lacking.

Prime Minister Churchill disagreed. He said that a major raid had to be made for several purposes. One was to answer the constant stream of Russian complaint regarding the failure of the Western Allies to open a second front. More important from a military point of view was undertaking a raid to show the difficulties involved. Without it, said Churchill, no responsible commander would undertake the planning of an invasion of Europe across the channel. Churchill discussed the need for a large-scale military operation with Lord Louis Mountbatten, the Chief of Combined Operations, and Mountbatten agreed that the only thing they could do on short notice was to carry out the Dieppe plan. Five thousand troops were committed to an action on the French coast.

General Montgomery was proved correct. The Germans were quite aware that an amphibious operation was being planned; after all, they had already attacked it once. Dieppe was the obvious place for it, and so they moved up reinforcements and made plans for a powerful defense. They could calculate as well as the British the best times in terms of weather and tides. One of the good times was between August 10 and August 19. When the British arrived on August 17, the Germans were ready for them.

Ostensibly the Canadians had limited objectives: to destroy some radar installations and gain some other information. Actually Dieppe was a sacrificial mission, and four-fifths of the men employed became casualties.

When it was all over, the British had learned a great deal, most of it negative, but all of it invaluable for the future.

They learned they did not have enough landing craft, and that the ones they had were not of the right kind. They had not appreciated the need for naval gun support and air support. The commandos had been trained superbly and were in excellent condition, but the organization of the amphibious raid was inept.

Out of Dieppe came a great truth: the invasion of Europe could succeed only if it comprised three major factors:

1. Security. The enemy must not know where the invasion was coming.
2. Surprise. The enemy must not know when the invasion was coming.
3. Concentration of force. The strength of the invasion must be mighty, and the enemy must not know how many troops were to be employed. The follow-up troops must move swiftly so that the foothold gained could be strengthened before the Germans had time to rush reinforcements to the area.

To accomplish this latter, it was soon seen that the major problems concerned the ports. The usable ports grouped themselves into two segments. On the one hand was the Pas de Calais area, where the invaders would have to get hold of either Le Havre or Antwerp. (The ports of Boulogne, Dunkirk, and Calais had been so badly damaged that they could be ruled out.) The alternative was to drive for Cherbourg, which would put the Allies onto the Cotentin Peninsula, which the Germans might seal off, creating a most unpleasant situation. Needless to say, the Germans had built mighty defenses at all these ports and could be expected to fight bitterly for them.

To resolve the difficulty, General Morgan assigned a team of American staff members to come up with a plan of assault against the Normandy area, and a British team to plan for the assault against the Pas de Calais. This was done, but it was still necessary to choose between them. The British advocates of Pas de Calais would not budge, nor would the advocates (American and some British) of Normandy. Beneath this quarrel were the opponents to any cross-channel attack at all, who for a time seemed to have won the day.

The problem was then attacked from a new direction by Lord Louis Mountbatten, who continued on as Chief of Combined Operations. Mountbatten had a peculiar position as a relative of the royal family and a debonair air which masked a bright and inquiring mind. He was known in the British military establishment as an enfant terrible for his unorthodox approaches to problems. This time he dragged the teams up to Scotland, where he maintained a headquarters at Largs, and forced them to talk over their various difficulties and listen to one another, instead of sitting up late at night writing negative reports.

Out of all this came an agreement that there would be a cross-channel attack. And from that, with a good deal of guidance from General Morgan, came the decision that the attack would be made against western Normandy rather than the Pas de Calais. This decision was made in June 1943, just a year before the fact, and the invasion then was projected for the end of May 1944.

And so, on July 15, 1943, the voluminous plan was completed and sent off to the British chiefs of staff. Since it was basically a British plan, it presupposed the predominance of the British army. The key point in the minds of the planners was Caen, the capital of Normandy. After Caen was taken, then the troops would wheel to the right into the Cotentin Peninsula and capture Cherbourg. In two weeks they should have Cherbourg, with forward elements at Mont St. Michel, Alencon, and Trouville. Further than that the planners could hardly plot; the enemy's reaction would have to be taken into consideration.

The British chiefs of staff considered the whole supreme command structure to be their own and the COSSAC plan to be theirs, too. The Americans on the staff warned time and again that if the British chiefs of staff went to a Combined Chiefs of Staff meeting and pulled out the Overlord plan as a fait accompli, then the fat would be in the fire, and the whole operation might collapse in the bonfire of a Combined Chiefs argument. Morgan wanted to send a delegation to present the plan to the Americans; the British chiefs objected, and Morgan got around it by sending a delegation of Americans on a less formal basis, proving that General Morgan knew of more than one way to skin a cat.

On August 3 the British chiefs of staff went off to the Quadrant Conference at Quebec. A British detachment of COSSAC went along, too, and briefed Prime Minister Churchill on the way aboard the *Queen Mary*. So when Prime Minister met President, they both had been given the benefit of briefings from elements of COSSAC. And so good a job of planning had COSSAC done that both political leaders accepted the commitment. Out of the conference came the decision that Operation Overlord was to be the major effort of the United States and Britain in 1944.

The plans then came up for implementation. It was estimated that by the end of 1943 nearly a million American servicemen would be in England. By March 1944, the figure would hit 1.25 million. But there were worries; one of the most serious was a perennial shortage of landing vessels and crews to man them; a new worry was security. Until this point security involved only the people of Norfolk House and the higher echelons of the British and American services. But bringing a million Americans into Britain and focusing the attention of the press on the project posed a whole new security problem. Security was to be the key problem in the whole of the invasion. General Morgan summed it up by saying that every chance of leakage had to be eliminated, if possible.

2

Enter
Eisenhower

IN THE spring of 1942 the Americans began pressing for a
second front in Europe, in accord with the decision arrived at by Prime
Minister Churchill and President Roosevelt at the Arcadia Conference the
previous December.

But where was that second front to be? General Marshall, the U.S. Army
chief of staff, assigned Brigadier General Dwight D. Eisenhower the task of
preparing an offensive strategy. Eisenhower had come up from Fort Sam
Houston, Texas, to be chief of the Army G-3, or Operations Section. Many
officers and political leaders on both sides of the Atlantic still believed the
adventure of crossing the channel was too risky. Eisenhower showed how, by
establishing overwhelming air superiority, the army forces could be ferried
across the channel and, given adequate naval support, could gain a foothold
there. This attitude represented General Marshall's own thinking, so it was
quickly approved by him, and then by his opposite numbers in the Joint
Chiefs of Staff, Admiral Ernest King of the navy and General H. H. Arnold of
the U.S. Army Air Forces. Marshall then took the plan to President Roosevelt, who approved it that very day and sent Marshall to London to present
the plan to Prime Minister Churchill and the British chiefs of staff.

In London the plan was also approved. But the British wanted the whole
plan shelved until 1943. The year 1942, which Roosevelt wanted to mark the
second front, was deemed impossible. Marshall admitted that it would *be*
impossible to achieve the level of troops, weapons, and ships to deliver them
before the last months of the year. And the last months of the year were the
time when nobody wanted to launch an invasion across the English Channel.
One good storm could destroy the whole operation.

The most important outcome of the Marshall visit to London that spring was the decision that the cross-channel assault was to be the primary offensive in Europe when its time came.

When General Marshall returned to Washington, almost immediately he sent Eisenhower to London to draw up a plan for the organization of American forces in Europe. Eisenhower spent ten days there and returned to give General Marshall a plan for unified command of all American forces in Europe. As it was with General Morgan, Eisenhower was writing his own ticket. A few days later he was appointed to command American forces in Europe.

What were these forces to do? As Marshall and Eisenhower now agreed, there was no chance of launching a major cross-channel attack in 1942. At the time that Eisenhower was appointed to this new post, Prime Minister Churchill happened to be in Washington, and there he learned that in North Africa General Rommel had just taken Tobruk from the British forces. The talk at the White House turned to the possibility of staging an amphibious operation against French North Africa to take the pressure off the British.

Before June was out, Major General Dwight D. Eisenhower had headed for Europe to assume command of the European Theater of Operations for the U.S. Army. His bases were in Britain and Iceland. His command consisted of two American divisions in Britain and some air force units in Northern Ireland. There was much talk about a second front, but virtually nothing with which to bring it about. The British, who really did not like the whole concept of a charge across the English Channel, had seen how slight was the American presence and used that as an argument against Operation Sledgehammer—the invasion of France. Even the first American air force operation against the Germans was not carried out until July 4. The British now began to give signs of wanting to reconsider the whole idea of the cross-channel attack. General Marshall was furious and he went to Admiral King, who all along had wanted to prosecute the war against Japan first. They agreed that in view of the British attitude this should be the course of the United States and took that plan to President Roosevelt.

But Roosevelt had committed himself in 1941 to turning American power first against the Germans, and he was not now convinced to the contrary. Instead of agreeing with them, the President sent Marshall and King to London with Harry Hopkins to try to work out details for Operation Sledgehammer, even if it turned out to be a temporary foothold on the European continent.

Marshall, King, and Harry Hopkins went to London and there they did argue, long and hard. The British flatly opposed an invasion of the Pas de Calais area. The German forces were much too strong, they said. And given the experience at Dieppe, where, even as the Anglo-American disputants met, the first invasion attempt was frustrated and the second was in the works, the British were quite right. General Marshall held out as long as he could for a cross-channel attack in Normandy, even after being persuaded that the bridgehead might be established and lost. The Soviets had said Russian morale was such that they might not be able to stay in the war unless they were given relief by way of a second front. In the final analysis, the Americans came around to the British viewpoint that it was going to take more time than was left in that year to prepare a successful invasion of Fortress Europe and that a potentially unsuccessful one ought not to be tried. On July 24 British and Americans agreed to Operation Torch, the invasion of Northwest Africa. Before Marshall went back to Washington that month, he appointed Eisenhower to command Operation Torch. The Soviets began to grumble again, as Marshall had known they would, but their grumbling was lowered in tone when the British Dieppe raid proved how disastrous an attempt to hit the continent could be without adequate preparation and forces.

Going from virtually no force at all in Europe to one capable of launching an invasion of Africa was a real task, but Eisenhower and his staff managed to pull off Operation Torch in November and December. It was a ragged performance, as anyone might have expected of the first American effort against the Germans and Italians, but it succeeded.

In the fall of 1943 the British and American views as to who must head the invasion of Fortress Europe diverged sharply. The Americans were more than ever opposed to "bogging down" in the Mediterranean, and the British showed time and again that they preferred to exploit that scene of action. It was known that Prime Minister Churchill still yearned to strike up through "the soft underbelly of Europe," which meant the Balkans from the Mediterranean. So the tension grew in a quiet way.

At the Cairo Conference Prime Minister Churchill was still showing the signs of his preoccupation with the Mediterranean, and the Americans were growing increasingly restless. On the eve of the conference, General Eisenhower's aide, Captain Harry Butcher, indicated that from conversations with Harry Hopkins it seemed the whole cross-channel invasion was still up in the air.

And if the invasion was to be on, as planned, then the Americans were now about to insist that the commander be an American, not a Briton. Eisenhower and the other American leaders were not a great deal more impressed with British military leadership than the British were with the American. At Cairo, among the Americans, the name of General Marshall was quite openly discussed as the commander of the invasion. Admiral Ernest J. King, the U.S. Navy chief of staff, said as much to Eisenhower at one dinner, indicating that the President would be appointing Eisenhower to become the army chief of staff when Marshall went to London to prepare. But the final decision as to who would command the invasion was not made at Cairo.

In the fall of 1943 General Morgan and a number of members of the COSSAC staff traveled to Washington to try to blast loose the appointment of a supreme commander for the Allied forces in Europe. It was generally accepted by this time in London, too, that it would be an American, and Morgan had rebuilt the COSSAC staff along American lines of command. Morgan and his party were wined, dined, and pleasantly treated, but still there was no appointment. Prime Minister Churchill had been given to believe it would be General George C. Marshall, the U.S. Army chief of staff, and so had virtually everyone else involved, including Presidential advisor Harry Hopkins and Secretary of War Stimson. But no appointment was forthcoming, and Morgan's party had to return to London empty-handed.

The most severe tensions were now building. It had become apparent to General Morgan that as the hundreds of thousands of Americans filtered into the British Isles and prepared for the channel crossing, the danger of tipping the Allied hand as to time, place, and power would grow. General Morgan's command recommended a ban on movement within England on a strip ten miles in depth from the coast from Land's End to the Wash, and from Dunbar to Arbroath in Scotland (excluding Edinburgh). The British chiefs of staff supported the idea. The British War Cabinet opposed it, as an example of the sort of infringement of civil liberties that the war was being fought to eliminate. And there the matter sat, with agreement only that it would have to be worked out with the supreme commander, once he was appointed. Until then, nothing could be done.

The COSSAC headquarters grew. The numbers of American units, troops, vehicles, ships, boats, and all else down to frying pans kept increasing, and yet there was no one in control. It was an almost impossible situation. General Morgan demanded the power to keep the muddle from becoming complete and finally got it. In the name of the still unchosen supreme commander he issued directives ordering the British 21st Army Group commander, the naval commander, and the air commander—all of them British officers—to begin the detailed planning for Operation Overlord. When the supreme commander was appointed, he would stake out an area of operation for the commanding general of the First United States Army Group. It was agreed that the 21st Army Group would concentrate on the Caen area (which the British believed the most important), and the Americans would operate on their right, at the base of the Cotentin Peninsula. The whole matter of command was fraught with dangers to the sensibilities of "Limeys" and "Yanks." It was agreed that except in emergency no British or U.S. unit smaller than a corps would be placed under the orders of a commander of another nationality. To please the British, President Roosevelt agreed to the appointment of General Bernard L. Montgomery not only as commander of the 21st Army Group, but as overall land commander of the invasion forces until such time as the supreme commander should establish his headquarters on French soil.

It was December before anything was done about the supreme command. While meeting with Prime Minister Churchill at the Cairo Conference, President Roosevelt decided that he could not spare Marshall, and the appointment had to go to Eisenhower. And so it was done.

In mid-December Churchill flew down to North Africa to confer with Eisenhower about a number of appointments that had to be made after the change. British General Sir Henry Maitland Wilson took over as Allied commander in the Mediterranean. Air Chief Marshal Arthur W. Tedder became Eisenhower's deputy in SHAEF. A new headquarters was established (and built) at Bushey Park, near Kingston on Thames, ten miles west of London. General Eisenhower arrived with his chief of staff, General Walter Bedell Smith, and General Morgan had to make the difficult transition of becoming deputy to Eisenhower's new chief of staff. The big change occurred on January 17, 1944. General Montgomery arrived, and not long afterward General Eisenhower brought General Omar N. Bradley in to be chief of the U.S. First Army Group. Supreme Headquarters, Allied Expeditionary Forces was established and began operating at top speed to prepare a landing on the coast of France within six months.

Morgan and his planners had accomplished a great deal. They were able to hand General Eisenhower a plan that called for attack across the channel by three assault divisions at dawn on May 5, with two more to follow up. Altogether, thirty-five divisions would be committed to Operation Overlord, fifteen of them British and Canadian and twenty American. The problem at hand was to get them ready to go within six months.

It took General Eisenhower a while just to digest the plan for Operation Overlord. There was also Operation Anvil, the attack planned against southern France. How was it to fit into the "Big Picture"? When Eisenhower had been commander in the Mediterranean, he had quite logically approached the war with that idea in hand, and had virtually promised the French that a major attack would be made in southern France. That promise had to be honored, and Eisenhower still believed in the idea, but the difficulty was equipment. As in the Pacific, the major problem lay in the number of naval craft available to land troops on a shore. As in the Pacific, the landings would have to be done in stages, so that the same landing craft and ships could be moved from one area to the other.

The problems of nationality that General Morgan had been able to slide over only by assuming a strongly pro-American stance, reemerged with the new appointments. General Smith, Eisenhower's new chief of staff, was an outspoken man and almost immediately got on the bad side of General Sir Alan Brooke, the chief of the Imperial General Staff, by arguing vigorously for the transfer of one or two people. This was not the British way, and the incident created more than a little difficulty.

Another vexing problem was the matter of command of air operations. It was all very well to have Air Chief Marshal Tedder as deputy SHAEF, but that did not control the troops. Air Chief Marshal Harris of Bomber Command had his own ideas, and he was strongly resistant to putting his forces under the supreme commander. He was backed by the British Air Ministry. So at the moment that Eisenhower took command, he did not have command of all aspects of the proposed invasion, and, in fact, he was never able to get it the way the Americans thought he ought to. Air Operations from the British Isles had been placed directly under the Combined Chiefs of Staff, who had agreed that the principal raison d'être of bombing was the destruction of German industry, and that was beyond the purview of SHAEF. The American airmen, General H. H. Arnold, chief of staff of the U.S. Army Air Forces, and General Spaatz of the United States Strategic Air Command, did not think much more of the use of their heavy bombers in direct support of troops than did the British.

With all this troubling the new command, work began at Bushey Park. By this time, January 1944, some 840,000 Americans had arrived in the British Isles and were stashed away in various corners, much to the delight of publicans and the dismay of British military men. "Overpaid, oversexed, and over 'ere" was the complaint of Tommie, who was paid far less and was too often overshadowed with the girls by the newcomers. That feeling was shared by many British officers, and some of them made their feelings known quite openly. In his diary naval aide Captain Harry Butcher recorded the reaction of one Briton so highly placed that Butcher did not want to name him. This gentleman had first aired his irritation with things American when Eisenhower was in the Mediterranean:

"Someone once called this war a 'phony' war . . . well, as thousands of Englishmen can see, the only part of this war being phony is your being appointed Commander in Chief of the Allied Forces in North Africa, when two of the finest generals (Montgomery and Alexander), having cleared the enemy from the Egyptian frontier to Tunis, take second place to someone whose only qualification is that he is an American . . ."

With Eisenhower's appointment as Supreme Commander Allied Forces, this gentleman reemerged to air a complaint that was heard here and there:

". . . If for some reason a British general was not desired we should have preferred a Russian general to lead the Allied Forces . . ."

Yes, anything but an American.

The irritation was mutual; General George S. Patton, in particular, never made any attempt to conceal his dislike and distrust of the British. General Morgan had certainly moved in the proper direction in setting up SHAEF in such a way that units were homogeneous at every level lower than the corps. Had it been otherwise, Operation Overlord might never have gotten off the British beaches. Patton often suggested that the Americans drive the British into the sea. The patience of Eisenhower and that of Prime Minister Churchill was often tried more severely by their friends than by their enemies. The British press was severely nationalistic in its approach, and so was the American. Almost immediately the status of General Montgomery caused difficulties. His 21st Army Group was British and Canadian. He was also commander of ground forces, until such time as Eisenhower established headquarters in France. That was a perfectly normal proposition; someone had to be in direct command at all times. But the American press suggested that Montgomery's position was a sop to the British, and the British press wishfully indicated that Montgomery was really going to be in charge, with Eisenhower as simply a political figurehead. Captain Butcher, reflecting on Eisenhower, was annoyed:

". . . I should think he would get sour on being written about as 'Chairman of the Board' and sometimes labeled 'timid' when he has had to do things which were so risky as to make some of his subordinates think him overbold, if not crazy."

Early in February Wes Gallagher, the Associated Press war correspondent who was a particular friend of Eisenhower's, came up from the Mediterranean. In a discussion of the bogdown that was then occurring on the Italian front, Gallagher suggested that it was because none of the generals (most of them British) would take the responsibility for action. What was needed, he said, was an Eisenhower to take the responsibility, then the others would have gone ahead.

In the fall of 1943 declarations from Moscow and Teheran indicated that the "second front" could not be far off. Generalfeldmarschall Gerd von

Rundstedt, commander of German forces in the West, wrote a long, pessimistic report for the German high command about the state of his defenses. He was anything but pleased with what had been done over the past three years. Up to the end of 1941 the only German fortifications on the French coast were seven heavy coastal batteries between Boulogne and Calais, a few naval coastal batteries, and some U-boat pens. In 1941, after the plan for the invasion of Britain was definitely scrapped, Hitler assumed a defensive, rather than offensive, stance in the West. The U-boat pens were magnificently fortified (the Allies never did manage to knock them out by bombing). The army, without much help from headquarters, because Hitler hated to think in terms of defense rather than offense, did begin to fortify the French coast. By the spring of 1942 the term Atlantic Wall indicated what was happening. The Soviets had staged their first winter offensive. The Americans had entered the war. The "on to Moscow" talk in Berlin had suddenly ceased. Hitler had to think seriously about his defenses. Fortunately for Hitler, Field Marshal von Rundstedt, who had earlier been relieved from the Russian front because of ill health, reported that he was recovered. Thankfully, Hitler had appointed von Rundstedt commander of the German forces in the West. Two weeks later, on March 23, 1942, Hitler laid down the plans for the defense of the West:

> In the days to come the coasts of Europe will be seriously exposed to the danger of enemy landings . . .
>
> . . . Timely recognition of the preparations, assembly and approach of the enemy for landing operation must be the goal of the intelligence service as well as that of continual reconnaissance by Navy and Luftwaffe. . . .
>
> . . . All available forces and equipment of the several services . . . will be committed by the responsible commander for the destruction of enemy transport facilities and invasion forces. That commitment must lead to the collapse of the enemy attack, before, if possible, but at the latest upon the actual landing.
>
> An immediate counterattack must annihilate landed enemy forces, or throw them back into the sea. All instruments of warfare are to be jointly committed toward that end.
>
> No headquarters and no unit may initiate a retrograde movement in such a situation. . . .

There it was, the Hitlerian declaration that the invading forces must be thrown back into the sea, and that no retreat would be tolerable.

The St. Nazaire and Dieppe raids had one unfortunate effect for the Allies. They convinced Hitler that the Germans must pour enormous energy into the strengthening of the Atlantic Wall. Dieppe, he maintained, was a major invasion attempt that had failed, only because of the timidity of the British local commanders. He called a meeting of his most important advisors on the West, Reich Marshal Goering, Reich Minister Albert Speer, who ran the Todt building organization, Field Marshal von Rundstedt, and a number of specialists. They met at the Chancellery and for three hours discussed the Wall. Hitler wanted 15,000 concrete strong points and 300,000 men along that wall. They would create an impervious defense ring. He wanted it all by May 1, 1943. Speer doubted if he could get 40 percent of it by that time. The work was begun. Representing the thinking of the most responsible German leaders, the work was concentrated in the Pas de Calais area. During 1942 four times as much concrete was allotted to that area as to the Normandy coast. One of the jobs of the Allies was to keep the ratio that way.

Along with the fortification, however, the Germans did not immediately increase the military strength in the West, largely because the demands of the Eastern war machine were insatiable. After von Rundstedt's gloomy report in the fall of 1943, however, Hitler ordered the strengthening of the West. Particularly impressive to the Allies was the appointment of Marshal Erwin Rommel to inspect the defenses. A few weeks later he was appointed to command Army Group B, under the authority of von Rundstedt. It was understood that it would be Rommel who would fight the battle against the invaders. As these changes came and were observed by intelligence, those who had spoken so blithely of a three-division invasion force became convinced that this would not be enough.

On both sides of the channel preparations were speeded up. On the German side, with the coming of Eisenhower to London the Germans knew that the invasion was approaching rapidly. Some expected it as early as February 1944.

Washington and London were also worrying. Eisenhower and his assistants were also concerned with the continued shortage of landing craft; it seemed to be developing as the bugaboo of Normandy. The shortage of LSTs was most troubling. These shallow draft ships were constructed so that the whole bow opened up, a ramp went down, and tanks and trucks could literally be driven ashore. They had proved themselves time and again in Africa and Sicily, Italy and the Pacific. The LST was the most valuable single landing vessel afloat, and the shortage was a real stopper.

From the moment that Eisenhower saw the first part of the plan for landing, he felt that it had to be broadened: more troops, more beaches. And that meant that the assault could not be mounted early in May but must wait at least until the end of the month. More troops had to be trained and practiced in landings. More assault craft had to be found somewhere. The British promised that somehow they would muddle through and produce their share of landing craft. The Americans sent a party from Washington, including General John E. Hull of the Operations Division of the army and Rear Admiral Charles M. Cooke, chief of planning for the navy and one of Admiral King's confidants. They talked for hours, and all agreed that the chief limiting factor was the shortage of LSTs. The May date for D-Day would have to be postponed at least a few days so that more LSTs would be available. Even this was going to be made possible only by further delaying the landing craft and ships available for Operation Anvil—the invasion of southern France.

By February, urged by the Americans and by Montgomery, the British chiefs of staff had agreed to an expansion of the beachhead to five divisions, instead of three. The new target date for the invasion was May 31, 1944.

3
Preparations for Invasion

MORE THAN a million Americans had to be brought into England to take their part in the great battle that was to begin in May. The first problem of the planners was to find a place for them, a strip along the seashore where they could train. It was finally found near the village of Appledore, and there the Assault Training Center was established. The engineers built a replica of a German strong point, a mile and a half square, studded with six-foot-thick concrete bunkers. Behind were four miles of beaches, which would be approached by landing craft.

General Bradley arrived and took up his dual command of the U.S. First Army and the First United States Army Group, with headquarters in a building on Bryanston Square in London. It was a command that no one but Eisenhower seemed to take very seriously, since everyone agreed that the British had outmaneuvered the Americans by getting control of the three operational commands (ground forces, navy, and air forces) while pushing Eisenhower to cloud nine. Thus, what would be the function of FUSAG and what would Bradley do?

He would train the American troops, for one thing. And then he would command them in battle. For it was never envisaged in Washington or at Eisenhower's headquarters, although it was gospel in London, that American troops would serve under British commanders for longer than a few days.

Bradley had two headquarters: the Bryanston Square FUSAG setup and First Army Headquarters at Bristol. His task was to prepare the American troops for their assault.

On January 23, 1944, the various SHAEF commanders all met together for the first time at Norfolk House and learned that the invasion force had been expanded from the original three divisions to five divisions. Inevitably the discussions came around at last to the question of the availability of landing craft. They could take Caen. They could take Cherbourg. But they could take these places quickly enough for them to be useful only if they could bring in enough troops—fast. That meant more landing craft. This discussion became sort of an intramural game, with everybody talking a great deal, but the actual progress appallingly slow. The landing craft that belonged to Operation Anvil were very much coveted. As Bradley later put it, "During the winter and early spring of 1944, Anvil led a frenetic, on-again off-again double life. . . ."

So desperate was the thinking at one point that the SHAEF planners suggested the deliberate overloading of landing craft. General Bradley and General Montgomery were quick to rise in objection; such a move might cause the whole landing operation to disintegrate.

Because of the landing craft shortage on March 21 came the decision to postpone Operation Anvil and defer the Normandy landings until June 1944.

Meanwhile, General Bradley had brought a small group of officers up to London from Bristol to make plans for the U.S. First Army, which would launch its invasion at the foot of the Cotentin Peninsula, with the striking forces of two army corps, V Corps and VII Corps. By February 25 the plan was complete. On D-Day the army would put 55,000 men from 200 units ashore.

The V Corps would land on the beach called Omaha. The VII Corps would land on Utah Beach. They would be followed up by XIX Corps, which would come into Omaha. The choice of commanders for these units indicated one of the most serious of the problems of the United States Army in World War II—an enormous need for capable and experienced officers that far outstripped the supply. Major General Leonard Gerow, commander of the V Corps, was a seasoned and capable officer in every since of the word. But Major General Roscoe B. Woodruff was assigned to command VII Corps, and Major General Willis D. Crittenberger was assigned to XIX Corps, and Eisenhower and Bradley both worried about these two officers. Neither was an experienced battle commander, and they would be "cutting their teeth" in the most important military operation of the war. That was no place for the training of generals. The decision was made to send one of them to the Pacific and the other to the Mediterranean to gain some experience in the art of war, while two experienced officers, Major General Lawton J. Collins (Guadalcanal) and Major General Charles H. Corlett (Kwajalein) took over VII Corps and XIX Corps respectively.

As the training and preparation continued, British-American amity was certainly no more than skin deep. Even the least choleric of American officers, General Bradley, used hard words. The success of his proposed landing on Utah beach would depend on the ability of the troops to get across the beach and past the marshland that lay between the beach and the farmers' fields. That marshland was crossed by several narrow causeways, and the Germans had flooded the marshes. As long as they held the causeways there was no way the Americans could get off the beaches. General Bradley asked for an airborne landing behind the beaches to capture and hold the causeways and seal off the neck of the Cotentin Peninsula so the Germans could not rush reinforcements in. All these views were aired at planning sessions in the headquarters of General Montgomery at St. Paul's School, outside London. Eisenhower knew of them through General Bedell Smith, his chief of staff. So did Air Chief Marshal Sir Trafford Leigh-Mallory, commander of the air forces for SHAEF. One day, after many discussions, Leigh-Mallory suddenly spoke up against the proposal. He could not approve, he said, it was much too dangerous, and the losses would be too high. That plan, he said, had to be scrapped.

Bradley's dander was up. All right, he said, they could scrap the airborne landings. They could also scrap the Utah Beach landing if they did.

Leigh-Mallory stared at him. Senior British officers were not used to arguments. He wanted to make it quite clear: if Bradley went ahead, it would be over Leigh-Mallory's opposition. He then turned to Montgomery and said that if Bradley insisted on going ahead, he would have to accept full responsibility.

Had this been a British meeting, the airborne invasion would have been cancelled at this point. "Accept full responsibility" in British English meant—if it doesn't work, you are in big trouble. But Bradley spoke up angrily again and said he was in the habit of accepting full responsibility for his actions.

Montgomery restored a semblance of order, rapping on the table and announcing that he would accept responsibility for the airborne operation.

That was how many discussions went, due to basic distrust between the two armies. After forty years, a reading of the official documents makes it possible to wonder how the invasion ever got away from Britain's shore intact. That it did is an enormous tribute to the patience of Eisenhower and Churchill, who stepped in time after time to intercede in bitter quarrels and to smooth ruffled feathers.

In the airborne landing dispute, Air Marshal Leigh-Mallory carried his opposition all the way to Eisenhower, not once, but twice. Eisenhower stood firmly for the operation.

At the highest echelons, the British continued to hold the American military in a sort of contempt. Field Marshal Sir Alan Brooke kept reminding acquaintainces that he fully expected disaster. Eisenhower had never commanded even a battalion in action.

"I had little confidence in his ability to handle the military situation confronting him, and he caused me great anxiety. Tactics, strategy, and command were never his strong points."

U.S. troops landing on the beaches would be the 1st Division, the 29th Division, and the 4th Division. Only the first of these was an experienced combat division; Big Red One had already led two invasions. But the 29th Division and the 4th Division were going to have to rely on training. And so they trained.

Throughout England the tension rose. General George S. Patton, well known to the Germans and much respected by them, was sending multifarious messages from his "headquarters" on the east coast of England. It was part of the Allies' masterful deception plan to fool the Germans into believing that the invasion would come at the Pas de Calais area. The Russians, told of the approximate day of D-Day, announced that they would stage a spring offensive at the same time. Prime Minister Churchill was holding meetings, pushing hard to achieve what was needed in terms of harbor devices and more landing craft.

The harbor devices—the most important of them—were themselves a product of Churchill's remarkable inventiveness. On May 30, 1942, he had sent along to Lord Mountbatten a note about the sort of artificial harbor that might be necessary for the invasion of France. Out of this, and the discussions in the COSSAC meetings, came the plan for two enormous artificial harbors, one for the British zone, and the other for the American zone.

In their thinking about the points of invasion of France, the Germans always came back to one problem of the enemy: he must have a port into which he could discharge cargo to maintain the furious pace of an invasion. And so they tended to think of the Pas de Calais, or even of the Belgian coast, two areas where the good harbors were located. All the while, the Allies had decided on Normandy and were making their dream come true.

If the artificial harbor was to be the key to successful landings on the Normandy beaches, then it must be a harbor the like of which had never been seen before. And that is what the engineers promised—the Mulberries.

They would consist of concrete caissons, over a mile for each Mulberry. These were called Phoenixes and would be sunk in line off the Normandy shore. To protect them from the pounding of the sea, floating steel tanks called

Bombardons would be moored three miles out. The unloading facilities, called Whales, consisted of floating piers which would rise and fall with the extreme tides of the Normandy beaches. These would be connected to the shore by floating roadways mounted on pontoons, which were anchored in the seabed.

The plans were begun before Eisenhower arrived. When the decision was made to assault with five divisions instead of three, that meant the Mulberries must be larger. So shelters for additional craft were to be provided by crescent-shaped breakwaters called Gooseberries. These were to be created by sailing merchant ships across the channel and scuttling them in the proper places. Besides the roadways, the Mulberries would come with Rhino ferries, lighter pontoons filled with air, which could be strung together to make rafts capable of carrying tanks and trucks ashore. The American requirement was for a port that would unload 5,000 tons a day, and the British needed even more, a facility to handle 7,000 tons.

On the eve of the Quebec Conference the plans were made, and the work was ready to proceed, but approval from the highest officials was needed, since the Mulberries would be the keys to success. Time was pressing. The Prime Minister was scheduled to sail on the *Queen Mary* for America to meet with President Roosevelt. So Lord Mountbatten set up a demonstration and lecture for the Prime Minister aboard the ship. It was held in the bathroom of the most luxurious of the ship's suites. The scientific advisor, Professor J. D. Bernal, gave the lecture. Standing on a toilet seat, Admiral Sir Dudley Pound, the First Sea Lord, compared the shallow end of the bathtub below him to a beachhead. Into the tub Bernal then floated a fleet of twenty ships made of folded newspaper. Lieutenant Commander D. A. Grant made waves with a back brush.

Disaster! The whole fleet sank. Grant then inflated a Mae West lifebelt and floated it in the tub. That, said Professor Bernal, represented a harbor. Grant placed a new fleet inside the Mae West and again made waves with his back brush.

The fleet did not sink!

And that is how the senior officers of the British empire were convinced of the essential soundness of the Mulberry plan.

The building of the Mulberries began. From the outset it was hard. It was a naval undertaking, but the navy did not have the technical knowledge to do the job, so the Royal Engineers did much of it. This created frictions within the British military establishment. One day Lieutenant General Sir Archibald Nye, vice chief of the British general staff, inquired as to the difficulties that kept popping up. He went to Sir Harold Wernher, who had been appointed coordinator.

"Why don't you coordinate?" he demanded.

"You can't coordinate people who refuse to be coordinated," said Wernher.

So the British muddled along, and the Mulberries proceeded, very slowly.

The invasion schedule called for a naval bombardment of the Normandy coast, so the experts conferred and decided: heavy bombardment for thirty-six hours.

On April 4, General Eisenhower inspected the 29th Division. He and General Bradley had agreed that morale was the biggest factor of all in the success or failure of the coming invasion, and those two generals visited hundreds of American units. Later Eisenhower made a trip to visit air stations housing B-26s, fighters, and B-27s. On April 7 General Montgomery staged a full-scale dress rehearsal of the invasion plan at St. Paul's School. Eisenhower and Churchill and the King of England all attended. A relief map of Normandy thirty feet wide had been spread out on the floor, and Montgomery, a good showman, tramped across the map showing how the troops would move.

Meanwhile, those troops were being tested. At SHAEF headquarters a map was set up showing the beaches on which U.S. forces would land. It showed gun emplacements, hedgehog defenses, barbed wire, and minefields. These were being reproduced in the training establishments along the English coast. In December 1943, a training area had been established in Start Bay and at Torbay. Full dress rehearsals were set up in late April and in May for the Omaha Beach and Utah Beach forces. The American troops were moved down from their camps in southwest England to concentration points much closer to the channel. Here they were issued the special equipment they would need, and they coated their vehicles with waterproofing to ward off the effects of salt water. Then the various units were moved to forward areas called "sausages" because of the shape on the map. They and the British separately would practice "invasion" in some ten divisional exercises. The coast of southern England was the American exercise site, south of the British naval base at Dartmouth, near the village of Slapton Sands. The geography here was quite similar to that Norman coastline across the channel. Slapton Sands itself was a beach of coarse gravel that reached out into a shallow lagoon. Above were grassy bluffs, almost the duplicates of those across the English Channel. All the adjacent villages had been evacuated. "Defense" troops were assembled, Americans and British who would play the roles of Germans and their allies and try to destroy the effectiveness of the landings. Air power would be brought in. Artillery was set up to fire and add to the realism. The "invaders" would be escorted by warships, and minesweepers would lead the way, just as it was going to be on D-Day on "The Far Shore" as the troops had come to call Normandy. The troops were to be taken out of their "sausages" and loaded aboard assault vessels and then landed at Slapton Sands as much as possible in the manner that the real landings would be carried out a few weeks later. Engineers and tanks would accompany the infantry, the engineers to clear paths through the obstacles and minefields, and the tanks to lend armored support against the Tiger and Panther tanks they expected to meet. So a large number of suitable vessels were assembled in the ports around Dartmouth. There were LCTs (Landing Craft Tank), the first of the craft of that sort, an invention of Winston Churchill's during World War I, flat-bottomed craft with hinged bow doors and a ramp. Some said there were too many of these—they were unstable and dangerous. By far the better instrument was the LST (Landing Ship, Tank), for it could travel at ten knots in rough water, carrying even LCTs, and, of course, tanks, and hundreds of soldiers.

There were also LSIs (Landing Ship, Infantry), which were mostly British and mostly converted civilian vessels. And there were LSDs (Landing Ship, Docks). There were also Landing Ship Gantrys, Landing Craft Assault, and Rhino ferries, which were 1400-ton steel rafts used to unload LSTs in deep water. And there were two huge artificial harbors, the Mulberries—but these would not be tested on Slapton Sands.

For months the British and American navies had been planning their part of the landing—Operation Neptune was the code name. American bases had been established in 1943 at Rosneath in Scotland and in North Devon at Bideford Bay. Both areas had the sandy beaches of the sort that would be encountered in Normandy. Admiral Sir Bertram Ramsay, Allied naval commander, counted his precious LSTs day by day. He was to have 900 LCVPs, 168 LSTs, and 241 LCIs. By mid-April he still did not have all of them. It was a worrisome time. Preparations for the invasion were warming up; Admiral Ramsay was just about to transfer his headquarters to Southwick House, a mansion seven miles north of Portsmouth dockyard. General Eisenhower was preparing to move into a trailer a mile away in a hazelnut grove, across the way from Montgomery in a similar trailer. Everyone sensed that time was fleeting. As the days rushed by it became apparent that the time for training was almost exhausted. All the troops had to be given one big exercise, with conditions made as near to those of the coming reality as possible. It was a dress rehearsal, this chance to learn by experience before they moved into the shot and shell from the German guns. Ten simulated landings: Operation Duck, Operation Parrot, Operation Beaver, Operation Tiger, six parts of Operation Fabius—and then the real one. The next step would be to the "hards," or concrete ramps, from which they would board landing vehicles, and the next step after that would be in France. Once the troops moved into the sausage-shaped confinement areas, their lives changed, for now they would be briefed on their mission, and the rest of the world was not to know.

That last was as important as all the rest. The world was not to know.

4

Putting It
All Together

FORGETTING FOR a moment the difficulties of common allies separated by a common language and uncommon usages, the differences in approach to such matters as supply and transportation between the British and Americans make it seem miraculous that the Normandy invasion ever left shore.

Nothing was the same. British lorries were American trucks. British small arms used a different size ammunition than American, as noted, and so did the big guns. Tanks were quite different. Even the five-gallon jerrycans carried two different sizes of gallons. Very wisely General Morgan and his planners decided at the outset that British and American forces would be kept as far from one another as possible. Of course, some adaptations were made by choice. Senior American officers adopted the practical British battle jacket, and it became standard. The jeep was ubiquitous, the finest general purpose vehicle of any army anywhere. But for the rest, tanks and trucks, howitzers and machine guns, each nationality tended to keep to its own. Britain had to produce more of the weapons she had been making all during the war so that they could be sent ashore with her men when the invasion came. America had to keep stockpiling supplies and continue bring over her ultimate force of 1,350,000 American troops, along with their organizational equipment and vehicles, from the United States to the United Kingdom. All that manpower and equipment would be brought to the European continent within ninety days after D-day. That meant ammunition, rations, clothing, fuel, lubricants, construction materials, and everything else an army needed, right down to toilet paper. The supply people had to get the stuff there, across beaches and through damaged ports. They had to be ready to repair and operate trains along damaged tracks and use ships and boats and roads quite unfamiliar to them. And while the assault troops were training, the logistics and supply men were learning where they were going and what they were going to do.

Until the fall of 1943, the supply and transportation sections operated under a loose directive with a very small staff headed by Colonel David W. Traub. He and the staff could only guess at what was going to be needed, based on their past experience and the projected troop strength of the theater. Not until the Operation Overlord plan was accepted that fall could any detailed work be done. It was February 1944 before the Services of Supply could draw plans for logistical operations on the continent during the three months that would immediately follow D-Day. That gave them three months to get ready for a vast operation.

The first plans called for the almost immediate use of the port of Cherbourg. And, of course, after the capture of a port and the securing of the beachheads, material could be ordered direct from the United States. But in the beginning it all had to come to Britain and then go out.

The magnitude of the task is indicated by the situation of a single truck company. It would operate forty 2½-ton trucks, each of which could move a five-ton payload. The logistics people could not agree on how many companies would be needed. Transport said 240 companies. G-4 (Supply) said 160 companies. SHAEF Movement and Transportation Division said the Transport men failed to back up their claims. The Transport men said they could not back up their claims because they were not given basic operational data, such as the plans for deployment of U.S. forces on the continent. And G-4 being SHAEF, the G-4 figure became fact: 160 companies, a matter that caused General Bradley trouble in the weeks to come.

From experience in North Africa the supply men knew that the 2½-ton truck did not do everything needed for movement of a modern army. They wanted bigger trucks, 28-foot semitrailers, 6x6 cab over engine trucks, and wide-bodied trucks. But back in Washington the supply people thought the channel fog must have gone to the supply men's heads, and the bureaucracy slowed everything down. It was months before the big trucks began to arrive. By spring, virtually none of them had. So the 2½-ton truck, with all its limitations, became the basic vehicle with which the American army moved through Europe, once again proving the adage that the generals are equipped to fight any war with the material of the last one.

Improvisation was the rule of the day. One way to increase the carrying capacity of the slender truck corps was to provide two drivers for every vehicle. Thus, each truck could operate twenty-four hours a day—until it broke down.

The Military Railway Division of the Transportation Corps also began preparing for action, but it was generally accepted that no usable locomotives would be captured for at least the first month after D-Day.

In September 1943, the southern part of England, south of a line between London and Bristol, began to bristle with encampments and installations. British forces concentrated in the southeast, and U.S. forces in the southwest. The concentration areas were about fifty miles from the point of embarkation. In January the Americans began mounting exercises; the first was Duck I, which involved the movement of troops into landing craft and an "assault" with naval and air support on the beach at Slapton Sands. The idea was to simulate the conditions in unloading supplies over a beach under the guns of the enemy, discharging cargo and handling various sorts of landing craft and vehicles. From the Sicily invasion came the idea of lashing supplies to small wooden platforms that could be handled by mechanized equipment or pulled over the beach like sleds.

The VII Corps arrived in England in October 1943. American naval forces were consolidated, and the American participation in the cross-channel assault was placed under Rear Admiral Alan G. Kirk. Rear Admiral John Wilkes was put in charge of securing and building landing craft for the invasion. Rear Admiral John L. Hall was appointed to supervise training of amphibious landing forces and then to command them in battle. He would take in Force O to Omaha beach. Rear Admiral Don P. Moon would take Force U to Utah Beach. On paper, British Admiral Ramsay was in charge of all this activity, but, in fact, he let the Americans very much alone to operate and train in their own way until the actual assault.

At first it was supposed that the American troops coming to England would arrive adequately trained for the cross-channel attack. But so many special problems arose that the work of the Assault Training Center became all important. Virtually all of the American troops scheduled for Operation Overlord were to be exposed to battle conditions here.

The U.S. 4th Infantry Division was the nucleus of Force U, which was to attack Utah Beach. The U.S. 1st Infantry Division was to lead Force O in the attack on Omaha Beach. Force B was built around the 29th Infantry Division and the followup troops (not dropped) of the 82nd Airborne Division and the 101st Airborne Division. All these troops and their supplies would be moved in 10 transports and 539 landing craft.

As for the 1st Division, it had begun its war in North Africa and come on from there. New unblooded units would need special training, but not these old hands.

General Bradley decided that every regiment of the 4th Division would go through the training course.

General Montgomery was planning to rely far more on his own troops than on the Americans. General Miles Dempsey's 2nd British Army was the key organization. Eight hundred and fifty thousand British, Canadian, and Polish troops would cross over to France, on the left of the 1,200,000 Americans. Three British divisions had seen action before, the 7th Armoured Division (the Desert Rats from North Africa), the 50th Infantry Division (Northumberland), and the 51st Highland Division. Montgomery was counting on these blooded troops, and the Germans also regarded them as the major threat. The fact, however, was that these three units had been fighting for too long a time. An old soldier is a careful soldier—that was the adage, and a careful soldier refrained from taking risks when he could. That kind of soldiering did not lead to lightning moves by an army. As it would turn out in Normandy, what the Americans lacked in combat experience they soon made up in enthusiasm. The experience was to come quickly enough.

Apart from inexperience, the really major American military deficiency, going into Normandy, was their tanks. The United States had concentrated on production of the Sherman tank, which, by German standards, was totally obsolete in 1939. The German 88 mm gun could knock out a Sherman before the American gunners could get into range with their smaller 37 mm and 75mm guns. But, as the Americans had already learned in Africa and Italy, even the Panther and Tiger tanks were easy victims for fighters mounting cannon.

All these factors were to some extent known to Allied intelligence, and in the spring of 1944 the training exercises concentrated on making the most of Allied power, and on overcoming the deficiencies in one way or another. The P-47 fighter, with its huge engine and heavy armament, had been brought to Europe as a high altitude fighter for escort of bombers. Actually, it had already been discovered that the P-47 was an excellent strafing plane, and in Normandy it would be used to counter the German tank superiority. By observing German defense works, the British and Americans had made some adaptations in their armored vehicles to make them more useful. One important change was the "crocodile"—a Churchill tank equipped with a flamethrower that had a range of 360 feet. The Crocodile towed a 400-gallon armored trailer. The other device was the "flail tank," an ordinary Sherman tank that turned a drum in front of the tank. Chains were attached to the drum, and they flailed the ground as the tank moved forward, exploding land mines as they went. All of these devices were to be part of the war games, the amphibious assault landings on the British shore that would top off the training of the troops for the great cross-channel adventure.

In the spring, army and navy intelligence watched the German buildup of defenses with an eye to countering them.

Most pleasing was the growing feeling that the Germans really believed the invasion would be launched against the Pas de Calais. In February 1943, Hitler and the German General Staff became seriously concerned about the paucity of accurate intelligence about the Allied plans.

From time to time Field Marshal von Rundstedt issued an appreciation of the current possibilities. Almost always it consisted of five factors:

1. The sea crossing must be short.
2. Maximum air cover must be maintained. Another argument for the shortest distance between England and France.
3. The landing place must be on the route to the heart of Germany.
4. The landing troops would have to destroy the sites of the new weapons the Germans had devised to bombard London—the V-1, and V-2 rockets.
5. And above all the Allies must take one major port.

Early in 1943 *Fremde Heere West* (Foreign Armies West), the army intelligence service covering the Western front, was taken over by Colonel Alexis Baron von Roenne, a Prussian officer whose predictions about the actions of France early in the war had proved accurate.

But because of a remarkable state of scheming within the German intelligence services in bidding for Hitler's trust, the number of Allied divisions for the invasion was completely misrepresented by the German intelligence services. For a time Hitler believed the Allies had so few divisions available that he was sending troops from France to the Eastern front. Then his intelligence men began doubling their estimates, and Hitler stopped that practice. The result, however, was that the Germans had no sensible concept of the strength of the Allied forces. Germany's unseen problem, with Heinrich Himmler seeking control of intelligence, and the navy and the army and Admiral Canaris's Abwehr all vying for prestige, was that there was no single coordinated central intelligence clearing house, no brake on the wildest of concepts and bitter rivalry within the system. The Allies could not have had more help from within the German system of intelligence if they had planned it.

At one point a fright was thrown into the SHAEF officials when someone observed that the beaches the Americans would be landing on were undoubtedly underlaid with peat. The conclusion was reached because similar beaches in the United Kingdom had a peat base. Peat beaches would not support heavy vehicles. The prospect of a beach full of mired vehicles was a worrisome one, so British commandos made night landings on Utah and Omaha beaches, dug down and collected a number of samples of the beach material. No peat. One more problem resolved.

Such dangerous missions were common. Only by close observation could the Allied forces have a good look at the sort of obstacles they would face. Between the spring of 1942 and the end of May 1944, Allied airmen photographed every foot of the French coast. Heavy bombers took pictures as they came over on other missions. Fighter bombers coming in to strafe took pictures of the coast line. Then there were special reconnaissance missions directed against the specific areas where the Allied troops would land, Gold, Juno, Sword, Omaha, and Utah beaches. After the end of December 1943, attention had to be paid to new obstacles being erected. When Field Marshal Rommel took charge of Army Group B, he began strengthening the Atlantic Wall, creating what he called his "devil's garden." There was only one way to see what he was doing—come and look. So aircraft and submarines took photographs, and commandos landed on the beaches by night, sometimes sawing off samples of metal defenses to see just what they were made of.

One of the worst obstacles was the antitank, antilanding craft defense that consisted of logs driven into the sand or set in concrete, with teller mines on top. These mines threatened the landing craft, the amphibious tanks, and tractors. Another was a barricade with a metal shoe on top, designed to rip open the side or bottom of a landing craft. The British went over to see them, came back and reconstructed them, and began figuring out methods of overcoming the problems. Prototypes were set up at Slapton Sands.

After much soul searching, it was decided in London that H-Hour would have to be at low tide in the daylight, low water because the beach obstacles were designed for best effect at high water, and daylight to give the naval bombarding forces a chance to hit home before the landings. And this, too, was to be practiced on Slapton Sands.

Tidal conditions were another problem. The experts studied the tides. The practitioners tried to put the troops through conditions as close to reality as possible. And it was apparent that the tidal conditions, plus the underwater obstacles, meant the best time for landing was three hours before high water. The planners soon realized that conditions on The Far Shore were such that separate H-Hours would have to be arranged for each beach.

By early spring most of these problems had been thrashed out, and the results were being tested at the Assault Training Center at Woolacombe. June 1 was the new projected D-Day. Fire support and air support were being integrated into the assault program, and the infantrymen were taught how to deal with them. Admiral Kirk's Western Naval Task Force would land the 4th Division on Utah Beach. The troops would be carried in modified transports, which would debouch the men eleven miles offshore into landing craft. LCVPs and LCAs would carry them into shore, about thirty men in each craft, and they would go in by waves.

All sorts of landing methods were tried at the Assault Training Center. For a while the naval forces thought it would be a good idea to use smokescreens to cover the landings. But trials showed that the smoke tended to confuse the assault troops, perhaps even more than the defenders, because the assaulting forces were not as familiar with the terrain. Smoke was abandoned. Speed was the answer—get moving, get the men ashore, and let them spread out.

The 4th Division and the other assault divisions were then streamlined for the task at hand. The support troop level was decreased, and the firepower increased. The rifle companies were organized in assault teams, with special equipment to deal with fortified spots. Each platoon was split into two assault sections, each with twenty-nine men and one officer. (That was the carrying capacity of one LCVP). The assault teams included rifle teams, a bazooka team, a flamethrowing team, a wirecutting team, a BAR team, a 60 mm mortar team, and a demolition team.

In addition to the two assault platoons in each company, the third platoon was given an 81 mm mortar and a heavy machine gun instead of a BAR. After the men were ashore, each platoon would reorganize into a normal rifle platoon.

A tank battalion would be attached to each infantry regiment, and it would lead the assault. Part of the tanks would move in on LCTs and land with the first wave of infantry. Some others were modified for amphibious work and were to be launched about three miles offshore to "swim" in.

It would be practiced from preliminary bombardment to air support to that first GI getting his feet wet. That was the purpose of the exercises to be held on Slapton Sands.

5

Security

IN THE fall of 1943 security became *the* major problem of the Allied forces operating in Great Britain.

As General Eisenhower wrote later:

> . . . one of the principle purposes of SHAEF Command was to keep secret the probable date of the invasion across the English Channel. We were certain that the Germans knew of our general intentions, and consequently we gave particular attention to the guarding of information on the only three points in which we could possibly hope to obtain some surprise. These were the date of the attack, the place of attack, and the strength of the attack. Our concern about these things was so great that the most stringent kind of orders prevailed and an elaborate system was set up in order to watch every angle from which a leak might occur . . .

With the shuffling of British and American troops from other theaters into the United Kingdom for the launching of the invasion against German-held Europe, all sorts of new security problems arose. Ultimately more than 800,000 British and Canadian troops and over 1,300,000 Americans were to be involved. To be sure, in the beginning only a few thousand needed to know virtually anything about the planning of the invasion, but as time went on, more and more men had to be let into parts of the secret. General Frederick Morgan recognized the security risk from the start, and the COSSAC staff set up an elaborate security operation to guard against enemy discovery of two key factors in the invasion: where, and when. With a nice appreciation for the never-ending problems of Allied amity, the basis of the system was called the Bigot procedure.

"Bigot procedure," wrote Colonel Charles C. Blakeney of the intelligence

(G-2) section, "is a system adopted to ensure that documents of the greatest secrecy, dealing with specific operational matters, are afforded a degree of security over and above that accorded by the classification MOST SECRET."

The number of Bigot documents was actually limited. Only those that mentioned where, when, or how many had to be Bigoted. As time went on, however, the pile got thick.

Such documents had to be opened personally by the Bigot addressed, or by some person authorized in writing. Thus, at least theoretically, no unauthorized person would ever see them.

And further, to confuse those who must be confused, in any communication referring to where or when the word Neptune was substituted for Overlord.

There were in fact twenty-eight agencies authorized to initiate Bigot documents, ranging from the office of Prime Minister Churchill's War Cabinet to the U.S. Office of War Information, and the British Ministry of War Transport. Most of these offices, however, were military commands, such as the Admiralty, the U.S. Joint Chiefs of Staff, the various Allied commanders in chief (air, ground, and sea), and, of course, SHAEF when it was established in 1944.

From time to time one Bigoted document would supersede another. Then the Secret Security Officer of the division involved and the officer who was entitled to receive Bigoted documents had to get together and burn the superseded document.

If by any chance a Bigoted document were to be lost, the most unholy racket would be raised and the foundations of various offices would be shaken. Both the person who issued the order and the security officer of the division where the loss occurred had to be informed. The latter would begin poking everywhere in that office, meanwhile informing security officers of the other divisions that might be concerned, especially the head of the division where the document was supposed to be. And then G-2 would be brought into the picture, and even the British police, if necessary.

In the beginning all went well enough. There were a certain number of scares, but they turned out to be no more than that. Every effort was made to avoid slipup: the Bigot files and documents were marked BIGOT in big red letters on the top right hand corner. Subordinates were warned to keep away from them. The documents were always enclosed in an envelope within an envelope, both addressed to the named person, and the inner envelope was also marked BIGOT in big letters on front and back. Only the BIGOT and anyone authorized by him in writing could even touch the envelopes, and if anyone had any questions there was an intelligence hotline to call.

In spite of all precautions, however, one day in March 1944, the United States Federal Bureau of Investigation (which was not on the list of Bigots) reported to the chief of U.S. Army Intelligence that a package containing a number of papers marked Secret, Most Secret, and BIGOT had broken open in an army mail sorting office in Chicago. After the package broke and spilled out the contents, a dozen people had seen and handled them. The package had been addressed to "The Ordnance Division G-4," but the place of address was that of a woman who lived in Chicago.

Army intelligence swung into action. Agents rushed to Chicago. A hot message went to SHAEF, and, as the British say, "the balloon went up." SHAEF G-2 descended on G-4, which descended on the Ordnance Division. No one knew anything about it. G-4 Ordnance had never received the documents.

In Chicago it looked like a case of espionage. The street address to which the documents were consigned was in the middle of a German district, and the woman who lived there was of German descent. The documents mentioned the time and place of the coming invasion and gave many details about the supply needs and plans for the buildup. With two months to concentrate defense buildup in a narrow section of the Normandy coast, Field Marshal Erwin Rommel could build defenses and bring in enough troops to make the area virtually impregnable.

The papers had originated in the office of the Chief of Ordnance Supply (G-4), and they were traced to Sergeant Thomas P. Kane, the chief clerk. He had sent them to the address of his sister in Chicago.

It seemed an open and shut case. But investigation proved the reverse. Kane held the highest of security classifications, and with good reason. He was hard working and heavily overworked. He was also just then worried about the health of his sister, who had recently informed him that she was sick. Working late at night, thinking about her, he had written her street address below the "TO: The Ordnance Division G-4," and the clerk who picked up the package had put it in the army post office instead of the secret SHAEF mail.

But all this information was weeks in emerging. Meanwhile, Sergeant Kane was under suspicion, and his sister's house was watched. All the postal employees who had been anywhere near the package were also watched. Even when the authorities were 99 percent convinced that all was well, the surveillance kept up until after D-Day.

That was just part of the security problem. One day Prime Minister Churchill sent a concerned note to General Eisenhower. A prominent military writer in England had circulated among some higher authorities in London an article about the forthcoming invasion of France. A look at the proposed article indicated that this writer knew the contents of the Overlord plan, the when and the where.

There was no question about the writer's loyalty. He had access to the highest levels of British and American military society and British political society as well. What had happened? Moving around the country, at various levels, the writer had spoken to dozens of people about military matters. He had never asked any specific questions about the invasion, but in the general discussions he had come up with the place and the time.

This letter from Churchill so distressed General Eisenhower that he put out a special directive:

"The Supreme Commander desires that all SHAEF General and Special Staff Division Chiefs issue a warning to all members of their Staffs against discussing any aspect of operations with people such as military writers, newspaper correspondents, or other visitors to military establishments, *who appear knowledgeable,* but who are not required by their duties to know anything of our plans and intentions. Steps are being taken for a similar warning to be issued to Government Departments in London."

What an order! It was impossible to carry out unless the officials simply refused to discuss the war with anyone outside the military establishment proper. And that is what some officers felt impelled to do, much to the disgust of the correspondents.

Meanwhile, the number of troops in England increased day after day and the security problem rose along with their numbers.

Everyone at SHAEF was constantly bedeviled with new worries about security, and such phrases as "loose lips sink ships" were common additions to interdepartmental correspondence.

General Eisenhower, by this time, had contracted an alliance with the divorced lady assigned him by the British as a driver, and some muttered to themselves that he was the greatest security risk of all. But no one dared say anything like that to the commander of the Allied expeditionary forces. As far as the British government was concerned, as long as there was no blackmail attempt—and there was not, Eisenhower's sex life was not a matter for security discussion. In fact, for the British, Eisenhower's relationship with Kay Summersby was a hidden asset.

No such wraps protected anyone of lesser importance. Generals were as much under the gun as buck privates. And one general, in particular, was soon to feel the lash.

As April moved along, and the invasion and its decisions neared, Eisenhower grew visibly more tired and nervous. Security was constantly on his mind. The Chicago postoffice flap had been a great shock, and by April not all the skeins of it had yet been unraveled.

In mid-April came a blow to General Eisenhower that involved an old friend and classmate, Major General Henry J. F. Miller. General Miller had been chief of the Air Material Command in the United States. He had come to England as Quartermaster of the U.S. Ninth Air Force, and as such he was a Bigot, with the secrets of the invasion in his hands.

On the night of April 18, 1944, General Miller attended a dinner party at Claridge's Hotel's restaurant in London, one of the most fashionable of dining salons, the sort of place that one of the master spies in an E. Philipps Oppenheim novel would be bound to frequent.

The dinner was given by Mrs. Sloan Colt. Other guests were General Osborn, Commander Gordon of the Royal Navy and his wife, several Red Cross ladies, a colonel, and General Edwin L. Sibert, assistant chief of staff and intelligence officer of the U.S. First Army Group, the almost nonexistent command.

General Sibert obviously was not entranced by General Miller.

"I sat one place from Gen. M. He was obviously intoxicated and continually argued with Mrs. Hall (ARC) about RC Club for the IX AF. . . ."

Those are not the words of a dear friend. Tip-offs are the pejorative "obviously intoxicated" (apparently intoxicated would have been kinder) and "continually argued" which indicates that General Miller was an extremely quarrelsome fellow, threatening the tranquility of the entire evening.

But worse . . .

"Three times I heard him name or imply the target date in no unmistakable [sic] terms in a voice loud enough to be heard by several other people at the table or by waiters. (This in the main dining room at Claridge's) . . ."

To be sure that he had it nailed properly, General Sibert went about as far as he could go.

"I afterwards asked Mrs. Hall if she was conscious of the significance of what she heard and she answered that she was. . . ."

Next morning General Sibert dashed off a handwritten letter to General Bradley, and Bradley shot it on to Eisenhower. Eisenhower rushed over to see General Carl Spaatz, who was General Miller's superior. General Miller denied that he had been intoxicated, and Eisenhower and Spaatz came to believe that contention. Nor was what General Miller had said as deadly as General Sibert had indicated. Miller had remarked more or less enigmatically that he expected to be on the other side in six weeks or so. That was hardly a giveaway of time or place. By that time, in April, everyone in England who had any knowledge of the war's affairs expected the same.

But, given the atmosphere that existed, much of it created by Eisenhower's own nervousness, immediate and strong action was indicated. This was particularly true, given the source of the complaint, one of the highest ranking intelligence officers. If Eisenhower failed to act directly and strongly, then the whole intelligence community might wonder how resolved on secrecy he really was. So, with hardly a tremor, as a commander must do, General Eisenhower shot down his old West Point buddy. He informed General Marshall in Washington of the security breach and asked for permission to reduce General Miller to his permanent army rank (colonel) and send him back to America. General Marshall granted the permission. Miller made a personal plea to Eisenhower to save at least his reputation by letting him go home as a general, but he was reduced, disgraced, and sent home. He was lucky not to be court-martialed. Some at SHAEF were insisting on it, but, even in extremis there is room for a bit of mercy. The medics conveniently found that he was suffering seriously from arthritis, and shortly after his return to the United States Colonel Miller was retired.

Was such strong action necessary?

General Eisenhower obviously believed it was. So conscious was he that he had but three hole cards in this coming battle—the where and the when and the how many of invasion—that nothing could stand in the way of their protection. Anyone who gave the slightest indication of threatening security had to be dealt with ruthlessly and swiftly. In that connection, General Sibert's question to the Red Cross ladies was also a threat to security, for it most certainly impressed on them the veracity of what they had heard. But even at SHAEF they could only go so far.

Actually, from the standpoint of real danger to the invasion, it seems unlikely that General Miller's remarks were a real threat.

Back in America there was indication that the SHAEF action was too harsh. A Canadian businessman later wrote Eisenhower to tell him how loose had been the talk in the Americas at the time.

"I want to point out that most of us knew invasion was planned for an early date this year; and we were certainly given plenty of information in this respect by the various radio stations. Also certain industrial developments are now taking place . . . which I am certain would not have been started if those in charge did not know the starting date of the invasion. . . .

"I have also been in headquarters and have had high-ranking officials come into my office discussing similar events which would have possibly involved a heavy loss had the enemy been able to adequately use this information. . . . Also some of the details discussed over long distance telephone come under this category.

"Therefore if this officer is to be penalized it would seem only right that the thousands of others who have committed similar indiscretions perhaps unwittingly, should also be penalized. But as this is impossible, sympathy should be extended to . . . Miller."

The logic of this argument was so indisputable that Eisenhower did not even reply to the letter.

Alex Johnson, the Canadian businessman, simply had no way of understanding that Eisenhower had no choice in the matter. Whether or not there was a single effective German agent in London (and David Kahn's account of Hitler's espionage system indicates there was not), the commander in chief had to behave as though his own office was infested and take any and all steps to preserve the three secrets that counted. Poor General Miller, certainly not the only man in England with loose lips, had to be sacrificed. He had made the dreadful error of committing his indiscretion in the hearing of an officer of G-2.

So, how far and where was SHAEF to go in preserving security. The answer was everywhere.

The threats to security continued, but so alert were the security forces that they were discovered and dealt with swiftly and effectively. Sometimes the results were almost comical. A British staff officer came in one night to report the loss, for reasons he could not guess, of the communications plan for Overlord, which contained, in a book the size of the Manhattan telephone directory, all the codes. But before G-2 could get into action, the lost property office of Scotland Yard called to report that papers marked BIGOT had been found in a briefcase left in a London taxi and turned in by the cabbie, who said with typical British calm that he thought they might be important.

So the luck of the Allies held. One reason it held so well was not known until after the end of the war. There simply was *no* German espionage apparatus left in England.

But there was still plenty of room for leaks, out of Ireland, a neutral nation virtually on the doorstep of the practice beaches, out of Lisbon, Stockholm, and Berne, which teemed with spies of all nations, and out of Washington, where security was so bad the British worried about it constantly.

The comings and goings of diplomats also worried SHAEF, and as the date of the invasion neared and practice operations and planning hit new peaks, Eisenhower asked the British government for those conditions requested by General Morgan months earlier: to limit travel, to declare certain areas of the United Kingdom off limits to citizens, to increase the control for the coming invasion. This time, Churchill was able to persuade the War Cabinet that with the invasion imminent, such stringent measures were acceptable. Foreign diplomats and their couriers were forbidden to leave the British Isles, and all incoming and outgoing diplomatic dispatches were subjected to censorship, in an unprecedented move by the British government. Also, travel to and from Eire and Northern Ireland was banned. This step had implications that the Germans could not miss, but it still did not say, when, where, or how many.

These measures were duly advertised to the troops, by Allied intelligence. Here is part of a memo from G-2 for the various commands:

> This unprecedented measure . . . was taken, as the British Foreign Office announced, to prevent "any inadvertent disclosure of information" which would result "in helping the enemy or in loss of British or Allied lives."
>
> Note the word "inadvertent." A neutral diplomat obviously would never intentionally divulge military secrets. Neither would any member of this headquarters intentionally help the enemy. It is, however, the inadvertent blabbing—about movements, about equipment; even about guesses as to when and where the blow will be struck—that does the damage. Stray scraps of gossip seemingly unrelated and unimportant by themselves can be added up by clever intelligence work into something big.
>
> These measures which have been taken by the allied governments will help in preventing leakage of military information. They cannot, however, be entirely successful in themselves. The best way to keep the enemy in the dark is for all of us, from general down to private, to refrain from talking.
>
> That's where you come in. . . .
>
> A.G. Sheen
> Lt. Col. GSC
> for Major-General A.C.of S.
> G-2 (Intelligence) Division.

Such severe and continual security measures could also be abused. Captain Edward Miles of the United States Navy apparently got on even less famously with his British counterparts than did many of the Americans. Out of the blue came a report from Air Chief Marshal Sir Trafford Leigh-Mallory, accusing Captain Miles of drinking too much at a party and then revealing Top Secret information. Miles denied it flatly and said he was the victim of an intrigue among the British. Eisenhower was in a real pickle; the complaint had come from his SHAEF Air Chief and could not be disregarded without a breach in Allied amity. Right or wrong, Captain Miles had to be sacrificed. So Captain Miles was sent back to the United States, where since the War of 1812 the admirals really had very little use for the British, and there his story was believed. He was sent to the Central Pacific, served with distinction in the Philippines and at Okinawa, held several postwar commands with distinction, and finally retired from the navy as a vice admiral.

The demands for secrecy had one serious negative effect: in mid-April General Eisenhower learned that staff officers at the divisional level were not being told what was going to happen, or when or where. Consequently, their planning for their divisional and regimental operations was ridiculously inadequate. The commander in chief was seriously upset by this failure, and SHAEF put out a new memo:

". . . while security must not be violated, it is equally important that all commanders, down to include the lowest on whom responsibility for planning devolves, must be clearly and completely informed of their own special tasks so that this work may proceed expeditiously.

"All commanders are charged with the responsibility of insuring that their subordinate commanders and staff officers are clearly and completely informed of their own special tasks. It is not necessary that all officers have complete information of operational plans. From the security point of view, it is highly undesirable that any officer should be unnecessarily informed of details other than those necessary for the efficient planning and execution of his own mission. In each echelon of command, subordinate commanders and staff engaged in planning will be assembled by groups, according to their responsibilities and common interests, and completely informed of all details necessary to each for a complete understanding of their own peculiar problems. Care will be exercised to insure that only those whose duties require it, and who are carried on the Bigot list are informed of target areas and dates. Opportunity will be taken at this time to again caution all officers of the extreme urgency of complete security, and the necessity for avoidance of discussion of any details of plans for operations or details of plans, for or of, the execution of exercises, with anyone other than those directly concerned."

One serious aspect of security in the spring of 1944 nearly brought a breach between the military and the civilian government. After much discussion between General Morgan's COSSAC staff it had been agreed that the delicate question of banning travel into or out of certain coastal areas around the time of the invasion would be left for General Eisenhower and the Prime Minister to decide. They did reach agreement that at the time of the invasion itself, it was certainly sensible to restrict civil movement. But when should civil movement and the ban on diplomatic communications be relaxed? That was the issue that divided Prime Minister Churchill's government and the officers of SHAEF. The British were very much put out, after the ban had been put down, to learn that various high-ranking and "important people" from the United States were moving in and out of Britain and the sensitive areas as though nothing were about to happen. When Robert McCormick, the editor and publisher of the *Chicago Tribune,* made such a trip, Churchill exploded. McCormick was known worldwide as an Anglophobe, and his newspaper had twice seriously compromised Allied war plans: once just before World War II, when it printed Plan Orange, the United States war plan against Japan, and after the Battle of Midway, when the newspaper announced that the U.S. Navy had broken the Japanese naval codes, a fact that could have destroyed the most important single element of the American intelligence system in the Pacific War. The British War Cabinet began jibbing again. Anthony Eden, the foreign secretary, argued that the British history of civil liberties must not be jeopardized by the military. Immediately after the invasion was launched, Eden said, the diplomatic and travel bans must be removed.

The military, however, had their own considerations, as expressed by General Eisenhower in a letter to Churchill:

> I have your note of the 27th May transmitting a minute by your Foreign Secretary of the 25th May, concerning relaxation of the ban imposed by you on diplomatic communications from this country, and with many regrets for the inconvenience that this may cause you, I fear that I cannot bring myself to agree with Mr. Eden's proposal as it stands.

> In my view and in that of all my principal subordinates, the lifting of the ban will indicate to the enemy that our major effort has at last been launched, and he will have the right to deduce that from that moment he is safe in concentrating his forces to repel the assault that we have made.

> As you know it has been one of my main preoccupations to persuade the enemy that our assault is to be made on a wider front than is in fact the case, and that our first assault is to be merely the preliminary to the main battle. I think that we have so far been reasonably successful in imposing this thought on the enemy command, and, for my part, I am extremely loath to surrender the advantage we have thus gained, unless this is absolutely unavoidable.

> It is possible that from other means at his disposal the enemy may appreciate that our NEPTUNE assault is in fact the main attack. If he does so, I think the fact will become apparent very quickly and I should then have no hesitation in recommending to you that the diplomatic ban be lifted at once and that other restrictive measures on the population be relaxed.

> I therefore ask you to consider the possibility of maintaining the diplomatic ban until such time as we shall have been able to appreciate the enemy's reaction to our first assault. It is possible that the inherent political difficulties might be mitigated if the foreign office should communicate with the Allied governments and Diplomatic Mission on D+1 or D+2 as he suggests, but to tell them that steps are being taken to afford them the relaxation they so urgently need at the earliest moment consistent with military requirements.

I suggest that we consider the matter together at about that time to see if then it is possible to fix a date that will not prejudice the requirements of military security. I do not however feel justified at this time, and before the battle is joined, in agreeing to any fixation of date.

The key to Allied success, as Churchill and Eisenhower had agreed all along, was to surprise the Germans, and keep them off balance long enough for the Allies to land two or three hundred thousand troops on The Far Shore, to get their supply system working, get off the beaches and onto land with room enough to turn around.

Eisenhower had never doubted the ability of the Allies to make the landings. What was at issue was their ability to make them stick. And to assure this, the commander in chief of SHAEF would do practically anything in the world.

6

Operation Deception

ONE KEY to the success of the Normandy landings had to be the deception operations that were building up on the southeastern coast of England, even as the U.S. 4th Division and all the other elements of the actual British and American landing forces were concentrating in the southwest.

The problem was primarily one of numbers. As the amphibious planners knew, it took about one-fifth the resources to mount an effective defense that it took to make an effective landing. And once the landing was secured, the Germans had the capability of moving troops from several areas to overwhelm the attackers.

In the fall of 1943 the COSSAC planners sat down to stare at the maps of the English Channel coast on The Far Shore. An invading army had to have supplies, and these had to be brought in quickly after the beachhead was taken, or the army might be thrown into the sea. Tanks, big guns, and heavy trucks were at serious risk when they came in by LST to the shore. How much better it was to have them brought up, along with thousands of tons of ammunition and supplies, to a dock and taken off in an orderly manner. But where were the ports? A look at the map of Normandy showed two major ports, Le Havre on the northeast and Cherbourg on the southwest. Both had been turned into fortresses by the Germans. Heavy shore guns protected both ports. The installations had been wired for demolition. Large concentrations of naval and army troops were located in both areas. If the Allies approached, the Germans would fight and then destroy the port facilities. It would be weeks, if not months, before they could be put in decent shape again.

This is precisely the discussion that was under way at Norfolk House in London on a summer's day in 1943, and it led to the actual building of the

Mulberry harbors. There must be a port in the first days of the invasion. Ten divisions had to be brought ashore by D+5, and thereafter a division had to be landed each day. Ten thousand tons of supply were needed for D-Day, by D+12 the need would be for 15,000 tons. By D+18, 18,000 tons of goods had to be brought in and every day after that an equal amount or more. If the Allies could not manage to take a port within the first few days and get it working, said the supply men, then they could forget about an invasion.

There was no way to forget it, said the line officers. The Prime Minister and President Roosevelt had ordered an invasion of France in 1944, and it was going to be brought off.

The supply officers and the line officers glared at one another across the table.

At this point, Commodore John Hughes-Hallett of the Royal Navy spoke up.

"Well, all I can say is, if we can't capture a port, we must take one with us."

Everyone laughed, and General Morgan adjourned the staff meeting. The next day, the commodore returned to the table with some facts and figures. After the difficulties suffered by the British in evacuating a quarter of a million men from the beaches at Dunkirk in 1940, Prime Minister Churchill had started an investigation of methods of connecting ship to shore in channel waters. Three years later the engineers had built a four-footed pier that could move up and down to adjust to strong tidal changes in the depth of the coastal water. An articulated pontoon pier to carry the traffic to the shore had also been devised. From these beginnings were born the Mulberry harbors, two huge concrete caissons, not unlike the usual concepts of Noah's Ark. Around them, to protect the Mulberry harbors from the ravages of the wind and waves, would be sunk the blockships. These would bear the brunt of the natural forces, and provide sheltered water where the ships could land their cargoes on the Mulberries.

After the demonstration aboard the *Queen Mary,* at the Quebec Conference, the British and Americans approved the idea of the Mulberry artificial harbors, and the work of building these monster structures began. Immediately a new security problem was posed; so many people were concerned with the various aspects of the artificial harbors that the danger of accidental exposure of the plan was enormous. The British managed to keep the secret, by offering any number of explanations for the strange building program. They were fittings for French ports, to replace destruction by the Germans, said one story. They were floating grain elevators, to be towed to Europe when the time came to feed the starving French, said another.

The more stories the better, said the SHAEF security men, just as long as none of the stories came near the truth: the Allies were indeed carrying their own harbors with them to France.

In the spring of 1944, the Germans were poised to face an invasion. They had a very good idea of when: late spring or early summer. But where? In 1943, Operation Starkey (the feint off the Kentish coast) had apparently failed to bother the Germans. In fact, it had convinced many high-ranking Germans that the ultimate invasion of France would come somewhere between the Somme River estuary and Dunkirk. Hitler almost alone suggested that the Allies might well invade in Normandy. He ordered the coastline there reinforced, and the work was begun. He ordered more troops to Normandy, and they were sent. But Field Marshal von Rundstedt, chief of the western forces, and Field Marshal Rommel, who held a more anomalous position as commander of Western defenses, were still convinced that Normandy was not the most likely place.

Hitler had changed his mind many times before; in 1941 he had said Normandy, at another time he had said Norway, at another time he had said the southwest coast of France.

His generals tended to believe that an attack in Normandy would be a feint and that the Pas de Calais area would be the site of the major battle for the Allied foothold. Further, Normandy might not be the only feint. From Italy the Allies could stage an invasion of the south of France as well. So the German high command had to watch a coastline of 1,200 miles, from the German border with Holland to the French border with Spain. The Germans maintained fifty-eight divisions in France, the Netherlands, and Belgium. Seventeen of these were located in the triangle between the Seine and the Loire rivers, twenty-five were stationed north of the Seine, and the rest were south of the Loire.

The German navy added a theory of its own, suggesting that there were six British divisions in Scotland, and that they might well be preparing to invade central Norway. That German navy belief did not come about by accident.

By the end of 1943 the watchword for the invasion of Fortress Europe was "Deception." Better than anyone else the British knew that deception was vital to their ends, and they had convinced the Americans and taught them some of the secrets of the trade. The British had been at it for years, beginning in Egypt in 1940.

By the time the United States entered the war, so sophisticated was the British deception system, that it boasted a command of its own, the London

Controlling Station. Colonel J. H. Bevan was the commander, and he worked directly under the Allied Combined Chiefs of Staff.

Before SHAEF was officially born, the Anglo-American Deception Unit came into being. It was formed under British Colonel Noel Wild. Its headquarters were in Norfolk House. Its task was to deceive the Germans as to the when and where of the invasion.

From the beginning, Colonel Wild was extremely fortunate in two respects:

1. British counterintelligence had captured all of the spies who operated in Britain, with the possible exception of some "neutral" diplomats. Use had been found for some of the spies of Admiral Canaris's Abwehr (German Military Intelligence). The British gave these agents the option of going to work as Double Agents, turning their services against their German employers. Some patriots had refused and were imprisoned or executed. Most had accepted to save their lives. They became essential factors in the game of deception, and their efforts were masterminded by the Double Cross Committee, a high-level interministerial organization in Britain, which Colonel Bevan ran.

2. Colonel Wild had at his disposal the Ultra system of decoding German military messages.

At the end of World War I the Germans learned ruefully that virtually all their codes had been broken by the British during the war. As they built the modern war machine of the 1930s, German army and navy officials were conscious of the need for total security in communications, and they set up a system that was supposed to give that security. It involved machine encipherment of messages. A machine called the Enigma machine was patented in 1919 in Germany and marketed as a means of safeguarding business secrets. It was not very successful, in a sales sense, although technically it was the most advanced secret communications method in the world. It used a system of wheels that moved each time a key was struck, and electrical currents. When the Nazis took power, they saw its usefulness immediately and bought up the patents. By the middle 1930s the system was in use in the Wehrmacht. The beauty of it was that anyone could learn to operate it, no particular skill was needed, and the machine itself was about the size of a portable typewriter. There were difficulties: the machine did not print out a coded text, instead each letter was lit up on a display screen so that two operators were needed, one to type the plain text and the other to copy down the code letters as they appeared. The machine itself consisted of five wheels, three of which were chosen for use at one time. Each wheel had an outer metal rim which could be locked into twenty-six different positions, one for each letter of the alphabet.

Every time the operator depressed a key the right hand wheel moved one space forward. Once every twenty-six times the middle wheel also moved, and as soon as the middle wheel had made its complete revolution, all three wheels moved together. The electrical current passed through the wheels and then back from a fixed drum by a different wire route. This routing could be changed by plugging pairs of plugs in any order wished. The positions of the wheels and the order of the plugs was changed frequently, and the operator chose different settings of the wheels for every message. All this was recorded by the operator in two groups of three letters each, with which every message began. Consulting his code books, the receiver then could set his wheels the same as the sender's. But the outsider faced permutations that totalled 150,000,000,000,000 possible different combinations. Knowing this, the Germans considered the Enigma machine absolutely foolproof and did not worry about the Allies' possible ability to break down the system. Once a message was encoded by an Enigma machine, the Germans had no qualms about sending it by wireless in ordinary Morse code.

Late in the 1930s the Polish government maintained an excellent intelligence system in Germany. The Poles learned of the Enigma system. The Poles knew they were high on the Nazi list for conquest, and they set about building an Enigma machine. They cooperated with the British and the French. Finally, just before the outbreak of war, the Poles managed to rebuild a damaged Enigma machine, and they gave it to the British. After war broke, the British set up a whole intelligence unit at Bletchley Park to work on a project called Ultra, which was nothing more or less than an assault on the German system of encoding through the use of the Enigma machine. By the summer of 1940 the British were reading German military messages. By the end of 1943 the expertise was much greater. One of the enormous values of this ability to read the enemy's mail was that the Double Cross Committee could check its results. If it sent out messages through the double agents to Berlin, and if the Germans reacted by sending messages to various military units telling them of the movement of American and British troops to this place or that, then the men encharged with the deception system could see that their plans were working. Obversely, if they failed, they could know that, too, and change their modus operandi. It was an enormous advantage to the Allies, and the Germans, certain they had perfected the machine that would keep their secrets, never suspected they might be fooled.

This enormous arrogance of the intelligence community was shared by both sides. The Germans did have undiscovered agents in the United States, Turkey, and other areas who worked so successfully that within weeks of the major high-level (Big Four) decisions on the conduct of the war, Berlin had its copies. The Germans knew, for example, that the Americans had accepted the need to defeat Germany before Japan. They knew that a second front was coming. They knew it would be staged across the English Channel. All this information was gained through espionage. One of the most successful agents was a German spy who was the butler to the British ambassador in Ankara. The British and the Americans were certain that their security was complete, but actually, it was not. David Kahn wrote in *Hitler's Spies,* that the Allied cryptological expertise denied the Germans any chance of breaking major Allied messages, but the fact was that the Germans tapped into Churchill's telephone conversations with President Roosevelt, they broke the British naval codes, and they had an excellent idea of what was going on across the channel. Their real problem was not a lack of information but too much, and conflicting, and it was here that the Double Cross Committee did much to save the secrets of D-Day from exposure and to prevent Hitler's forces from waiting in overwhelming strength at the tops of the Normandy beaches.

For more than two years, the Germans had been building the Atlantic Wall. Since the shortest distance between England and France lay from Dover across the strait of Calais —Pas de Calais in French—it was here that a sensible attacker would launch his invasion. It was here that the Germans first built their defenses. But in 1942 Hitler suddenly came to the conclusion that the enemy would arrive at the foot of the Cotentin Peninsula in Normandy, and the emphasis of defense on the channel coast was shifted there. Hitler soon was off on another flight, but he kept coming back to the Brittany Normandy idea often enough to keep a certain attention focused there.

On November 19, 1943, Field Marshal von Rundstedt noted that the Allies had by this time made very thorough military preparations for their invasion. A study of the Allied order of battle indicated that there were enough troops, enough ships, enough planes, enough of everything for the Allies to invade at any time. "Where he will come we do not know; neither do we know when he will come."

Those words were very welcome to the Allied security officers. Their goal was to keep it that way.

The great deception plan began on the morning of January 3, 1944, when Colonel Wild and Colonel Bevan met in the conference room at 58 St. James's Street, London, with the members of the Double Cross Committee, to secure the backing of that group in the greatest program of deception yet undertaken. They explained the problem: the Germans knew a great deal about the Allied plans and there were only two secrets that could be kept: where the Allies would invade and when they would invade. These secrets could be best kept by convincing the enemy that the Allies would invade someplace that they would not and at a time when they would not. It was as simple and as complicated as that.

The two colonels emerged from the meeting with the support of the Double Cross Committee, and the greatest deception of the war was on. It would have many facets, and would involve many people, performing sometimes apparently useless and even silly tasks. But if they were successful the result could be the saving of thousands of lives and even the success or failure of the cross-channel attack that everyone knew was coming.

In an analysis of the invasion prospects drawn up on October 28, 1943, Field Marshal von Rundstedt said the channel coast, the French Riviera, and the Bay of Biscay were the probable points of assault. This posed a most improbable defense plan, for it meant far more than a thousand miles of coastline to be defended. And what troops were to be placed where?

Hitler added to the feelings of confusion and impotence a few days later in a directive that spoke of the danger of attack in the West, but came to no specific conclusions. Both of these communications became known to the Allies through Ultra interception. The problem of deception then, was to convince Hitler, von Rundstedt, and all the others possible, that the invasion was going to be where and when it was not.

The Germans were working hard to ferret out the secrets, and they already knew a great deal. A transcript obtained through a German agent on the Swiss General Staff had given them the inside story of the Arcadia Conference of 1941 in Washington and a preview of the land offensives the Allies would launch against Germany in the next two years. Now, information secured in Washington, in Portugal, and other countries told the Germans that the invasion was coming, and that its name was to be Operation Overlord. The most important part of that information had come out of the safe of the British ambassador to Turkey on December 14, 1943, in a copy of a transcript of the Teheran Conference at which the final decision about Operation Overlord was made. Fortunately, the high-level-Allied planners had not concerned themselves with where or when. Equally fortunately, the Germans were suspicious, and Hitler, in particular, failed to appreciate the value of what he had.

The deceivers intended to get enough truthful information into the hands of the Germans so that they would believe the untruths that followed. For example, on January 15, 1944, the Abwehr office in Hamburg had a message from a young Danish industrialist in England. His name was Hans Hansen. He was a German spy. The message announced that General Eisenhower, who had disappeared from North Africa at the end of the year, would arrive in England on January 16. This was perfectly true and it confirmed to the Abwehr the fact that the British and Americans were preparing to launch the invasion of Fortress Europe soon. The German intelligence system had a "scoop."

And it had been handed to them by the British, through the double agent, Hans Hansen, turned by the British to work against the Abwehr.

This message was the sort of intelligence that impressed the Germans mightily. The truth of it was shown forty-eight hours later when the official announcement came that Eisenhower had arrived in England and that the Supreme Headquarters of Allied Expeditionary Forces had been established there. But actually what good had the timing of the information done the Germans? None at all. The German intelligence officers were like media editors; the fact that it was news was most important. The question of whether or not it was meaningful news got lost in the shuffle. As a result, despite the "scoop" of this agent, the Germans knew no more about the twin questions, where and when, than they had known before. On the heels of this "information" came the news that Air Chief Marshal Tedder was to be Eisenhower's chief of staff, and that General Omar Bradley was to be commander of the American forces. Again, big news, but what good did it do the Germans?

The deception campaign was beginning to unfold. Hans Hansen and the other trusted agents were setting the German intelligence apparatus up for the greatest surprise of all. Through an intricate combination of simple truth and inspired falsehood, they were going to lead the Germans astray during the crucial hours just before and just after the invasion.

One of the major efforts of the great deception campaign was a series of multifaceted operations called Operation Bodyguard, after a statement of Churchill's: ". . . in wartime truth is so precious that she should always be attended by a bodyguard of lies."

Operation Bodyguard was an immensely complex program, using virtually every aspect of British intelligence. It involved dozens of efforts, but the major ones were Operation Fortitude and Operation Zeppelin.

Operation Fortitude was actually three Operations Fortitude. Fortitude was intended to mislead the Germans about where the invasion would take place.

1. Fortitude North was the phony plan for the invasion of Norway; it also involved pushing Sweden into the war on the Allied side. After that, with Russian help, the Allies would invade Germany through Denmark.

2. Fortitude South, much more important in a way, was the fictitious invasion against the channel coast of Belgium —east of the Pas de Calais.

3. Fortitude South II. This was an extensive plan to persuade the Germans that the major invasion would be *after* a first strike, and the real invasion might be at the Pas de Calais or farther east. This was a short-range deception and long-range one —that is, it would continue *after* the Normandy landings and would encourage the Germans to believe that the first landing was still no more than a feint.

Zeppelin was a deception effort tied into a different part of Europe. It was designed to persuade the Germans that the British and the Russians would attack in Rumania to cut off the Ploesti oil fields, and that the British and Americans would also attack at Trieste, at the head of the Adriatric Sea, and move up through the Austrian Alps. At the same time the British would attack in Greece.

To Germans who knew the British thinking, Operation Zeppelin had a particularly dangerous sound, for this was the plan that the British really had wanted to follow.

Some indication of the effect of the preliminary disinformation campaign was indicated in an order put forth by Hitler. The Allies were already invading, he said, the first part of their invasion had come at Anzio. That whole operation was an attempt to tie down German troops as far away from the English Channel as possible. The statement was accompanied by a good deal of Hitlerian rhetoric about the enemy's attempts to destroy European civilization, but the fact was that the disinformation campaign was working at the highest level.

The German naval evaluation of March 5 stating that there might be as many as six British divisions in Scotland ready for some sort of operation in central or southern Norway was no idle error. The Double Cross Committee was operating in close conjunction with the commandos. The German heavy water plant at Rjukan had been blown up in a commando raid on February 20. The British were using radio and other methods in this part of the deception plan, called Fortitude North, to suggest just what the German navy believed. The Germans had stationed half a million troops in Norway with two Panzer armies and a large number of Luftwaffe elements. The British wanted to be sure they stayed up there, so they adopted a number of methods. First, they used the "turned" German agents to feed information to German intelligence about projected allied operations in the north. By January, one whole section of British MI 5 was turned over to the deception process. They were using forty turned agents to sluice information into Germany, just enough truth to make it plausible, just enough falsehood to mislead the Germans as to time and place.

To the Norway operation, which haunted Hitler, they added the possibility of a Soviet invasion as well. Until the orders came through stopping the movement of diplomatic messages, they also fed false information to Swedish and Spanish diplomats who were known to be friendly to the Germans.

Operation Skye was created to establish a phony army in the north. The commander in chief was General Sir Andrew Thorne. In fact, he did nothing at all.

A fictitious British Fourth Army was "assigned" to Scotland and given an enormous volume of radio traffic. An equally fictitious American Fourteenth Army was dreamed up. Colonel R. M. MacLeod set up "headquarters" in the dungeon section of Edinburgh Castle. He also had a "Corps" at Stirling and another "Corps" at Dundee. From these places about sixty people spent their days fabricating messages in the style of the British and the Americans suggesting corps, division, regiment, and higher headquarters activity. The Germans, familiar with the Allied orders of battle and methods of communication, recognized an armored division, an armored brigade, an airborne division, four infantry divisions, and two corps headquarters. They duly added these to the Allied order of battle. Operation Skye apparently would involve a quarter of a million men. According to the radio traffic, it even had its own tactical air force. Altogether, three hundred people, mostly retired military and women, made up complicated messages dealing with maintenance of vehicles in supercold weather, the relative merits of various ski bindings, and all the traffic relative to personnel changes, promotions, and unit movements that went into a real operation.

The Germans still believed they had successful agents in the United Kingdom. They had gone to enormous trouble to make sure this was so. For example: a Polish officer named Hubert had fought the Germans in Poland until the defeat in 1939. Then he had fled to France and fought the Germans again. After the fall of France he went underground and soon became the leader of a large group. He was betrayed to the Germans in 1942 by a woman and was there propositioned by the German Abwehr intelligence organization to go to Britain as a spy. If he went to Britain, the Abwehr promised, his underground associates would be set free. If he refused, he and they would be executed—not by the military, but by the Gestapo, which probably meant tortured as well.

Hubert accepted the offer and signed a contract with the Abwehr. The intelligence organization then arranged his "escape." He went to the underground, which moved him to England. On arrival in London, Hubert went immediately to the British authorities and told all. When MI 5 got onto the matter, they saw how valuable Hubert could be. Actually, he wanted to fight, and he was assigned to a Polish RAF squadron with the rank of wing commander. But MI 5 used his name and the codes and facilities the Germans had set up for him as Brutus to manufacture all sorts of stories for the German espionage service. Hubert actually never knew what Brutus was doing. Eventually MI 5 had "Brutus" posted as liaison officer of the Polish General Staff at the headquarters of American General Omar Bradley in London. There was a coup for the Abwehr—getting a man into the high councils of the Allied war effort! But, of course, neither Brutus as such nor the job ever existed. It was all a part of the ploy to feed disinformation to the Germans about the coming invasion. Brutus's particular mission was to indicate to the Germans that General Bradley would remain in England after the initial invasion of France under General Montgomery, and that Bradley would then mount the main assault in the Pas de Calais area. Since a growing number of German officials had convinced themselves that the Pas de Calais was the real target of the invasion, Brutus found an exceedingly appreciative audience in Berlin, one that was even more appreciative when the Double Cross authorities boldly transferred Brutus from Bradley's headquarters to a high liaison post with General Eisenhower, a mythical transfer of which the general was blissfully unaware.

Another master spy of the Double Cross system was Lily Serguiev, a highborn Russian woman who had left her homeland after the Bolshevik revolution, came to France with her family and became a French citizen. In her travels as a youngster she had met Felix Dassel, a free-lance "journalist." Later she ran into him when he had joined forces with the Nazis and was recruiting for the Abwehr. Through Dassel, Ms. Serguiev met Major Emil Kliemann, the number two officer of the Abwehr in France, and he fell for her. In the course of their romance she maneuvered a position as an agent under the cover name of Tramp, and in 1943 she got herself shipped to England by way of Madrid. That is, she got herself shipped by the Germans to Madrid and then walked into the British embassy and told all. Whereupon the British shipped her to England. She had the gall to return soon to Europe, to meet with Major Kliemann in Lisbon. From him she acquired a special German radio set to transmit her reports to Berlin, and after she returned to London she soon was sending reports back to Germany, all of them twisted to show that the main Allied effort was not going to be in Normandy.

Brutus and Tramp were agents of one sort, totally loyal to the Allies. They had sought the dangerous game of playing with the Abwehr. But there was another sort of double agent, the real Abwehr agent who had been caught. The fact was that all of the Abwehr's agents had been caught very early in the war, but some were continued in operation to the end, fed minor truths and great falsehoods, to keep the Germans happy with their intelligence system. Queries came from Germany about the powerful Allied forces assembling in

Scotland, and double agents confirmed that it was so. There were tales of Soviet officers seen on the streets of Edinburgh. The command at Stirling was the British II Corps, the agents informed Berlin. The command at Dundee was VII Corps. Newspapers and radio cooperated fully, although not always knowingly. Clippings about football games between "Fourth Army" units were sent to Germany. One day the local Scottish radio carried "the concert of a bagpipe band of the Fourth Army at a retreat at Edinburgh Castle."

The Soviets also leaked disinformation to the Germans concerning this operation. They let it be known that Soviet troops, transports, and a naval task force were preparing at Kola Inlet in the Barents Sea for an attack on Finland, a movement which was to begin in June.

The British commandos lent a real air of war to the proceedings. They attacked an oil refinery on the Norwegian coast. They mined the battleship *Tirpitz,* located in a Norwegian fjord. They sank ships and attacked a troop ship. They carried out campaigns against Norwegian railroads and roads. Planes flew numerous useless photographic missions along the Norwegian coast. All of this activity was a part of Fortitude North, convincing evidence that the British were planning action against the Germans in Norway.

In March von Rundstedt was suggesting that the invasion might come as a feint in the south of France, followed by invasion across the channel a few days later.

As April came, with the really heavy movement of troops in the southwestern part of England, the matter of deception in southeastern England grew even more important. If the reality was not to rouse the Germans, something must be done to draw attention elsewhere, and it was. Patton's new "Allied force" began operations in the south of England.

When General George S. Patton arrived in England early in 1944, the Germans began to speculate that he would play an important role in the invasion. Ultra intercepts indicated that, and Double Cross was quick to oblige the Germans in their line of thinking. Patton was the most logical of candidates. His campaigns in North Africa and Sicily had made him one of the handful of American generals the German general staff respected. It seemed to them inconceivable that Patton would not be employed in this greatest of battles.

In fact, Patton was to be employed. He was to command the U.S. Third Army, which would move through the U.S. First Army after the beachhead was established and would then drive for Paris. But at the moment, Patton was given the command of Bradley's First Army Group, an organization which did not exist except on paper. Landing craft were lined up in the Thames and the Medway and other streams and estuaries of the southeast shores of England. Steam could be seen coming up from their stacks, and vehicle tracks abounded in the parking areas. A number of large military camps sprang up, complete with barracks, trucks, and tanks. Tank tracks were seen by the German aerial observers, moving around from place to place, an indication that the British were carrying out large-scale maneuvers. The fact was that the tank tracks were made by dragging metal behind trucks, the landing craft were made of plastic and plywood and cloth, the barracks were constructed of camouflage materials. It was fakery, on a grand scale, but to the Germans who came over in their bombers and snapped pictures, it was a living, pulsing "army group."

To match the visual effect, the British dreamed up the aural. A large army group would be sending many messages to guide the units, and this happened day and night. The traffic indicated a large buildup opposite the Pas de Calais.

The Germans certainly took note. Ultra —which had opened a window into German high command planning—learned that on January 9 the Germans were taking cognizance of the activity of Patton's "army group." Patton came under discussion by the Germans that spring. A situation report indicated that his forces would be a great threat to the German 15th Army group in the Pas de Calais area.

At sea, the naval forces made sure the Germans saw a good deal of activity opposite that part of the French coast. Three naval squadrons were assigned to a deception operation. Their most important activity would come on D-Day, but long before they moved around the coast, giving the impression of an eagerness to begin the move to the Pas de Calais.

A.3725, which was the Abwehr file number of Hans Hansen, the Dane, was asked by his German superiors to find out what was going on in the Dover area, where the British and Americans were building up a false image of an enormous invasion force under General George S. Patton. Dutifully, Hans Hansen "went to the area" and reported back that he had mingled with two divisions of Canadians at Wye, with the U.S. 83rd Division at Ashford, and with the U.S. First Army Group headquarters at Folkestone. According to the many reports of agent A.3725, all through southeastern England, he had seen dozens of trains crowded with soldiers. There was no doubt that something big was building in the Dover area. Hans Hansen did not go so far as to say that he had become intimate with General Patton, but he did mention several generals by name, and one captain of the Royal Navy, and a high RAF official.

More departments of deception were operated by Britain's MI 6, and Special Operations Executive, with assistance from the newcomers of the American Office of Strategic Services.

This sort of operation, sometimes called "the department of dirty tricks" was a specialty of the British. Over four years of war they had perfected it. It was known that the Germans had studded the whole channel coast with excellent radio detection centers and radar installations. How could these be rendered ineffective? To find out, the British conducted a series of raids on the coast, captured a number of German radio and radar installations, and set them up on a deserted section of the Scottish coast. Amphibious and air units then made repeated "attacks and landings" against these detection units, and by trial and error developed means of fooling them. Aircraft and ships and shore stations installed jamming apparatus, to blind the enemy radar. The RAF made plans to fly over the Calais area on D-Day and drop metallic foil which would show up on the German radar as flights of planes. This foil should confuse the Luftwaffe into action. Two of the naval squadrons practicing along the Kentish coast would steam to the French coast and jam the German radar. They would also launch small foil craft, which would show up on the German radar as warships. These could be dropped over the side of a ship in "formations," or could be towed. Their effect would be that of a large formation of ships approaching the coast. At the same time, planes would be dropping their foil strips, and rockets would fire missiles containing foil to explode directly over the German radar establishments.

Another element of deception involved the airborne troops. Three divisions of paratroops and glider troops were to be dropped in Normandy, around Caen and in the interior of the Cotentin Peninsula, to block that area off and provide Allied access to the causeways from the shore. A dummy paratroop drop was planned for the same time in the Pas de Calais area. It was so elaborate a scheme that it had a name of its own: Operation Titanic.

Hundreds of dummies were made and fitted out in paratroop uniforms. They were rigged up so that when they hit the ground, the impact detonated "battle simulators," devices which produced the sounds of small arms fire, and of grenades and mortar rounds exploding. Smoke went up, and the aircraft that dropped the dummies also dropped bombs that fired flares up into the night and made more racket. In tests the British discovered that for half an hour they could thus produce the indications of a firefight. And a half hour of that at a time when all hell *seemed* to be breaking loose over the Pas de Calais coast and at sea—but actually *was* at Normandy—could be very valuable indeed.

In April, all was going well. The heavy concentration on security had prevented any dreadful breaches of the three secrets. But there were other secrets almost as precious, and one of them was that projected use of the Mulberry artificial harbors. If the Germans knew what those enormous caissons and the two huge "office buildings" moored off Tilbury really were, then they could concentrate their air power on the bulky structures as they crossed the channel and sink them.

By allowing so many stories about the structures to proliferate, the authorities kept interest in the huge construction plan (2.5 miles of concrete caissons) at a minimum. But the Mulberries themselves, those two huge structures as tall as office buildings, had to attract attention. German reconnaissance planes photographed them a number of times at their moorings off Tilbury. Obviously, those photographs went to Berlin and were studied by the experts. Would the Germans understand what they were seeing?

On April 21, 1944, the British traitor William Joyce, who broadcast for the Germans under the name Lord Haw Haw, announced that the Germans knew precisely what those structures were.

"You think you are going to sink them on our coasts in the assault," he said. "We'll save you the trouble. When you come to get under way, we're going to sink them for you."

For a few days London and SHAEF headquarters were in a flap. If the Germans knew so much, there was trouble ahead. But then Baron Hiroshi Oshima, the Japanese ambassador to Berlin, was taken on a tour of the Atlantic Wall by General von Rundstedt, who told him all about the massive concrete structures seen by the German pilots. They were, said von Rundstedt, antiaircraft gun towers. Baron Oshima wirelessed his report to Tokyo, it was intercepted and decoded and translated by the Ultra experts, and London breathed again. The secret of the Mulberries had not been appreciated by the enemy.

The invasion troops were by this time almost all moved down into the concentration areas in the southwest. They were shifting into the "sausages." They were very near the "hards"—the concrete ramps, where the troops would move aboard their landing craft. A whole division had been taken apart to provide service troops to meet the needs of the marshaling areas. From this point on the troops would be sequestered behind barbed wire. No more pub crawls. No more leaves to London. Civilian traffic in the coastal area was halted, and checkpoints were strung all across England, increasing the nervousness felt up to the cabinet level about the restriction on the freedom of the people. But the secret of D-Day had to be kept, and there was no other way. More than two thousand U.S. Counterintelligence Corps agents were detailed to prevent security leaks on the American side, and an equally large army of security men worked for the British. The Allies were approaching the most dangerous phase, the trial assaults, the final exercises, that would mean the bunching of landing craft, the movement of war ships, and the "invasion" of beaches.

It was all done with great skill. The "sausage" areas had been so well camouflaged that the Germans did not become aware of their significance. The concentration of troops in the southwest seemed to be matched by the concentrations in Patton's area of the southeast and by the frenetic "movements" in the north.

As the preparations for D-Day in Normandy were rushed along, so also did the deception plan increase in tempo. For two years, the British had been building one special network devoted to Operation Fortitude. It was the Garbo ring.

Garbo was the Double Cross Committee's name for the German spy V.319, who had been caught in February 1942, in England. His real name was Luis Calvo, and he was a Spanish newspaper correspondent, a cover for his activity as head of the Abwehr's Spanish group in England.

Once Calvo was captured, he was given the usual choice of collaborating or dying and he chose to collaborate. Actually, the British did not need him for very much, for they immediately manufactured a completely false "ring" with Garbo as the center of it. The ring apparently operated with ease throughout Britain. It included some twenty "agents," enlisted by Garbo, all of them fictitious, ranging from businessmen, to pilot officers of the RAF, hoteliers, traveling salesmen, and students, all of whom might have some reason for travel in a wartime Britain. Over two years the Double Cross Committee built up this espionage "ring" in the eyes of the Germans until by the spring of 1944 "Garbo" and his "agents" had earned the confidence of the Abwehr, who called the whole ring the Arabal Network. Arabal that April was furiously drumming into Germany the information that the Pas de Calais was the focal point of the major invasion, but that the Germans would have to expect subsidiary attacks in Norway, the south of France, and "perhaps" in Normandy.

Thus in the last days of April, with less than six weeks to go, in spite of the enormous difficulties of massing millions of men and millions of tons of equipment and thousands of ships for the invasion, Operation Overlord was yet a kept secret.

7

Operation
Tiger

FROM THE beginning of the planning for the invasion of Europe, British and American forces recognized the difficulties of joint operations, given the naval and military systems and traditions of the two nations, apparently so similar, but actually so different. The training period, beginning in January, would not only be for the troops who would land, but for the naval forces that would escort them across the English Channel, deliver them to The Far Shore, and protect the landings. The British and American land forces would operate independently of one another, but British and American naval forces would have to combine operations to put the men ashore and protect them in the process.

The first problem was to find an area deserted enough that it could be turned over to the military with a minimum of dislocation of civilian population. Just such a place was discovered in Devon, on the southwest coast. It was admirable because the terrain was remarkably similar to the Normandy beaches, where the actual landings would occur, and because it was relatively deserted. In 1939, the Royal Sands Hotel, a resort on the seafront at Slapton, had already been closed "for the duration" and evacuated. It was boarded up and as lonely as anyone could want. The engineers would have to deal with mines the British had sown on the beaches in their anticipation of a German invasion in the summer of 1940. Six of those had been accidentally exploded by a local farmer's dog who had ventured onto the beach. The result was not only the death of the dog, but so much damage to the hotel that it looked as though it had been in a war. And, of course, mines remained on the beaches. But the engineers could be trusted to put all that to rights, and if there were to be mines laid for the coming exercises, they would be laid in the proper places.

As far as the hotel was concerned, it would make a nice target for naval gunners.

In November 1943, the British government moved to take possession of the land. The War Office notified the Devon County Council that the area was being requisitioned for military use under the defense regulations, and that all civilians had to be out by December 20. Meetings were then held at the castle in Exeter, and they resulted in a vast bureaucratic plan to evacuate 30,000 acres of land, parts of six parishes. This meant the closure of 180 farms and many shops and small businesses and the relocation of 3,000 people from 750 families in a triangle whose base ran from Torcross to Blackpool Sands, with the apex at Blackawton. It included the villages of Torcross, Slapton, Strete, Blackawton, East Allington, Sherford, Stokenham, and Chillington. Everything—farm equipment, machinery, animals, furniture—was to be removed in six weeks. The Royal Navy would set up information centers to answer the thousands of questions involved, and the navy would also provide housing for the army of officials who would come down to supervise the evacuation.

At the first meeting, representatives of various voluntary organizations and of the local governments were informed. To ease the shock on the people, a second meeting of clergymen was called. They would be the buffer between government and the citizens, whose whole lives were suddenly being yanked out from under them.

The government representatives were as gentle as they knew how to be. Every expense would be paid by HM Government. All help would be given to find temporary accommodation for those affected. Rents would be paid, free storage would be granted for their possessions, and everything would be brought back at the proper time at government expense. Compensation would be paid for all damages. Still, no one could be expected to be very happy about being uprooted, even in the middle of a war, and so the clergy had a job to do, in a hurry. The military wanted the property almost immediately so that it could be transformed into as close a replica as possible of the Normandy beaches on which the Allied troops would land before midyear.

By the first of the year, the civilians were gone, and military men scurried about the deserted area, transforming it from rural landscape to military encampment, with blockhouses and bunkers scattered along the shoulders of the uplands facing the sea. Agents and aircraft had been supplying the intelligence sections with information about German defenses on The Far Shore for years, and these maps, plans, and photographs were now brought up to date and used to create as close a likeness of German Normandy as was possible.

British Vice Admiral R. Leatham, at Devonport, was the officer in charge of the Plymouth command, which had responsibility for the landing exercises. In the spirit of cooperation that was promoted in the SHAEF organization, it was established that from the time of leaving port, the American officer in charge of the task force carrying the landing forces was in tactical command of the force, including the British vessels that formed the escort. In so saying, Admiral Leatham specifically mentioned the possibility of attack by U-boats, aircraft, or E-boats, which were long, slim, highly powered motor boats, similar to the American PT boats. If such an attack occurred, the American commander was to deal with it as he saw fit.

In fact, no such attacks did occur in the early operations around the southern English waters. There were air raids, of course, but there were always air raids, and they seemed to be staged more for nuisance value than as an indication that the Germans were aware of any impending movement. The purely naval exercises and amphibious exercises went off, not without hitches—of those there were plenty—but without enemy interference.

The first of these amphibious exercises was Operation Duck which was scheduled for December 28, 1943.

One key unit assigned to the Utah Beach landings was the 1st Engineer Special Brigade, just returned from the Italian campaign to take part in the Normandy operation. Its commander was Colonel Eugene Caffey. Its strength was then about 3,500 men, but for the invasion it was to be increased greatly by addition of attached personnel. On Utah Beach it was anticipated that the brigade would number over 15,000 men.

The brigade had been back in England for just three weeks when it was called on to participate in Operation Duck. All its special equipment had been left behind in Italy, so a hurry-up job of reequipping was undertaken, and one beach group was gotten ready for the exercise.

After Duck, the brigade was attached to VII Corps and took part in several of that force's exercises, while VII Corps's own beach groups were training.

With the impatience of the experienced, Colonel Caffey and his men considered the exercises a waste of time. "In spite of the time consumed, by the exercises, the Brigade was able to carry on intensive training of its units in their basic missions. . . ."

The areas in which most practice was needed were cargo handling and supply dump operation. Coasting vessels were loaded with supplies and unloaded time and again over beaches in Cornwall.

On April 1, Admiral Sir Bertram H. Ramsay, commander of the Allied Naval Expeditionary Force, assumed command of the Western Naval Task Force. The Allies were getting ready to go into battle.

The next exercise at Slapton Sands was Operation Beaver. It involved the 4th Infantry Division and the 101st Airborne Division. At 4 A.M. on March 29 the 101st troops "jumped" behind the beach. Actually, they did not jump. On March 26 and March 27 the airborne troops were brought to their final staging area and briefed. Then they were taken to the "drop zones" by truck. They called the exercise "the GMC jump." The 502nd Airborne Infantry, for example, was to capture the causeway bridges leading inland (just as it would be doing during the real invasion a few weeks later). The 502nd was to secure the north flank of the bridgehead, while the 506th Airborne Infantry took the south side. Then troops of the 4th Division landed at 9 A.M. on a beach made to simulate Utah Beach where they would land in the real invasion. They were supposed to move inland across Dartmoor and to capture "Cherbourg," which was actually Okehampton. A naval bombardment preceded the seaborne invasion, and live ammunition was used. The Royal Sands Hotel was designated as "enemy headquarters" and took a beating at the hands of the naval gunners.

Despite the enthusiasm of the naval gunners, Operation Beaver was a great disappointment to all concerned. The navy and the army and the airborne all got confused. Units separated and failed to perform their missions. Afterwards, a series of conferences was held to try to iron out the difficulties. The success or failure of this learning lesson was to be tested in another operation, Operation Tiger, to be held at the end of the month.

Some units, such as the 1st Engineer Special Brigade, were growing weary of exercises since Operation Beaver was their fourteenth. The officers and men listened to the critiques, but they had heard most of the criticisms many times, and they said there were aspects to an "exercise" that could hardly be taken seriously. When the real thing came along, said the engineers, then the performance would be a lot different.

April 1 and 2 were devoted to these critiques of Exercise Beaver. Plans for Tiger were under consideration by Rear Admiral Don P. Moon, the commander of Force U, which would deliver the American troops to Utah Beach at the base of the Cotentin Peninsula in Normandy.

On April 3, American Rear Admiral Arthur D. Struble journeyed to Plymouth to confer with all the assault force commanders about the final exercises that would test the troop readiness and the ability of the forces of the two navies to cooperate effectively in the coming battle of France.

On April 7 General Collins's VII Corps headquarters issued the orders for Operation Tiger. The United States troops involved would be the 4th Infantry Division, the 101st Airborne and 82nd Airborne divisions, the 1st Engineer Special Brigade, and naval and air force units.

The purpose of the exercise was to "concentrate, marshal, and embark troops" in the Tor Bay–Plymouth area, for a short sea voyage, under the U.S. Navy, disembarking with naval and air support at Slapton Sands, using live ammunition. The troops would secure a beachhead and advance inland. The exercise would continue for three days.

The 4th Division would seize a bridgehead and drive inland. The 101st Airborne Division would land before dawn on D-Day west of Slapton Sands, and advance southeast to link up with the 4th Division. The 82nd Airborne Division would land on the east.

On April 10, Captain G. B. Dowling, the chief medical officer of Admiral Kirk's command, went up to the medical facility at Fowey, to conduct Exercise Splint. Even the corpsmen and the doctors and nurses were getting a taste of the future.

On the afternoon of April 13, the Navy's 2nd Beach Battalion exhibited its demolition techniques in exercises at Pentewan.

More personnel kept moving in. More conferences were held. On April 17 Admiral Struble was in Plymouth inspecting the facilities aboard the command ship USS *Augusta*. The *Augusta* was the flagship of the task force, and it would deliver the 4th Division to Slapton Sands for its final exercise before the landings in Normandy.

On April 18 the final plans for Operation Tiger were issued to all concerned. Even at this date changes had to be made. Some errors were found in the orders for small boat movement.

It was explained, ad infinitum as far as the engineers were concerned. In Operation Tiger, the higher authorities would see how well the American troops had been trained. It would involve the simulated landing of the United States Army 4th Division and supporting forces, scheduled in a few weeks to make the real landings on Utah Beach. The exercise would be conducted in that specially prepared area off the Devon coast, and there the troops would go ashore, attack inland objectives and would fight their way against "enemy" who were situated in positions which intelligence said were approximately those of the Germans across the channel.

On April 20 Undersecretary of State Edward L. Stettinius visited various encampments. He saw troops of the 101st Airborne Division preparing for the operation, and for the benefit of the press expressed his amazement at their competence. This was more or less standard order of procedure for the string of important visitors who moved through England that spring.

On April 22 the movement of the 4th Division and attached troops to the marshaling area began. This was D-5. The operation was committed.

On April 22 various unit commanders journeyed to South Brent, where Major General R. O. Barton, commander of the 4th Division, conducted a briefing. He laid out the invasion plan for them:

The VII Corps sector of the invasion front was located in the southwestern corner of Devonshire. The coastline was irregular, being interrupted by frequent exits of streams. On both sides of Slapton Sands the coast was abrupt and rocky, just as it would be on The Far Shore when the troops made the attack landing a few weeks later.

Very much like the Norman coast, the interior here consisted of many valleys and ridges, numerous streams, but none of sufficient width to cause serious trouble. Offshore from the village of Slapton was a raised beach about two hundred yards wide. On the seaward side it consisted of loose sand, small pebbles, and shingle. The tidal variation was about fifteen feet. Inland for thirty yards from the high tide line lay a beach of rough sand, which then leveled out to become twenty yards of sand and grass leading to a road ten yards wide. The beach then sloped gradually for twenty-five yards to the Slapton Ley, which was a landlocked basin varying in width from a hundred to three hundred yards. Two marshy streams drained into the Slapton Ley. Behind the country was hilly, and corridors would afford good cover if the high ground could be taken. Small patches of woods could be used to conceal vehicles. Hedgerows and farm buildings made for good concealment. Maneuvering off the roads would be hard because the roads were either sunk below the level of the countryside or deeply ditched, but that was how it was going to be in Normandy, too.

For the purposes of this exercise, the coastal sector between the mouth of the River Avon and Exmouth was held by the "German" 715th Infantry Division. The intelligence men went into the "history" of the unit as they did with the real German units in France: This division had been formed in April 1941, in this area. The commander was Generalleutnant Kurt Hoffman. It originally consisted of the 725th and 735th Infantry, but in 1943 another regiment, made up of Georgian (Russian) troops had been added. Defenses consisted of strong points on the beach and company and battalion headquarters inland. Strong points extended along the beach in the Slapton Sands area. They varied in strength from half a platoon to a platoon with heavy weapons including antitank guns. The Germans had established interlocking fields of fire, and all adjacent strong points were mutually supporting. Alternative points had been prepared for all infantry weapons—that meant mortars, machine guns, and the antitank guns. At night or during times of poor visibility continuous patroling was done between strong points.

The pillboxes were tank turrets mounted on concrete structures. The walls and roofs varied from three feet thick to six feet thick. (This was the way it would be in France.) Underwater obstacles were to be found at various places. Hedgehogs, tetrahedrons (built of steel) and steel piles were being installed on the beach just below the low tide level. Wire and minefields had been placed just above the high water line, north of the Slapton Ley, and covering the lower cliffs, which might be scaled. Roadblocks had been established at all beach exits.

West of the Avon River, the coast was defended by the 719th Infantry Division, and coastal batteries and divisional artillery were established there. The 719th Infantry Division had also been formed in 1941, the troops learned. It consisted of the 723rd and 743rd Infantry regiments, plus another regiment of foreign troops. Also included were the 663rd Artillery Regiment, and the 719th Engineer Battalion. Its commander was Generalleutnant Erich Hocker.

The village of Salcombe was "a small port with important logistical installations." Many of its buildings were "fortified."

The 242nd Infantry Division was known to be in the Plymouth area. This division had been formed in Belgium in the summer of 1943 and transferred to this area. It consisted of three infantry regiments. Its commander was Generalleutnant Flottmann. Two Panzer battalions were also known to be there. Other Panzer battalions were somewhere about, some equipped with French tanks, some with German Tiger tanks.

And besides these, possible dangers could come from a battalion of the 725th Infantry at Chagford, the 338th Infantry Division at Week St. Mary. The 338th Infantry Division was a crack organization, considered an offensive menace. It had an artillery regiment, a reconnaissance battalion, an antitank battalion, and its artillery and trains were believed to be motorized. From the Plymouth–Okehampton, Torquay area could come a parachute division, another panzer division, an infantry division and two Panzer battalions.

Extensive air support from the Luftwaffe had to be assumed.

All this, of course was imaginary, but the "German" situation resembled very closely what the Americans knew to be the situation of the actual German forces in the Utah Beach area: second-rate troops on the beaches, with the danger of first-rate units behind.

Hitler had ordained that the Allies were to be thrown into the sea, and, so

General Barton noted, the Americans had to expect a rigid defense on the beaches and attempts to reinforce the beach area. Counterattacks had to be assumed, as well as the arrival of airborne reinforcements for the enemy.

Thus, the 4th Division would have to reconnoiter to discover what the enemy intentions were going to be. The engineers would have to collect information on the roads, bridges, and obstacles. But before they could do that the 1106 Engineer Combat Group would send in assault teams to clear the beach obstacles and blow up the beach wall to permit passage of combat vehicles. They would also build an additional bridge across the Slapton Ley.

All the troops would carry with them one D ration and one K ration. Each unit would also carry three days of C or K rations, and these were to be the initial supply, just as it would be in combat. Rations brought to the beach were for emergency use only. All organizations would carry in a two-day supply of water in containers, on the basis of a half gallon per man per day. That was just how it was going to be in Normandy. In fact the operation included provision for collection of "prisoners of war" (American troops playing the enemy role) and evacuation of simulated casualties, who would be taken back out to the naval craft and held until the end of the operation. They even had simulated burials in mind, and cemeteries were designated.

The next day the navy and army commanders conferred with Brigadier General Elwood Quesada, chief of the Ninth Air Force Support Command. He would be responsible for fighter support of the actual landings and the simulated action for practice during Operation Tiger.

Three on-call missions had been allotted to VII Corps on D-Day and the next two days to mark the front lines with colored smoke. Besides that, on D-Day the 4th Division would have three request missions and three planned missions. The purpose was to interdict enemy reserves from moving up.

That same day, April 23, the advanced details of the 101st Airborne Division left their base for Torquay.

On April 24 the naval officers involved were also briefed at the Royal Marine Barracks Theater in Plymouth. The briefing lasted all morning and most of the afternoon. Meanwhile, the troops were moving toward the dock areas.

Troop movement to the dock areas left much to be desired. The vehicle drivers were not familiar with distance maintenance rules and vehicles jammed up on the roads. Part of the exercise was to "be bombed" by enemy planes on the way to the docks, and the "bombs," dropped at two areas around Plymouth would have been effective indeed. At the moment of one "bombing," thirty-seven vehicles were jammed together at the dock area. Had it been a real bombing they would have been destroyed or damaged. Thirty minutes after the bombing the engineers arrived and along came the ordnance recovery units, the wrecks were cleared away, and the roads repaired. If it had been real, the delay would have been about three hours.

Before the embarkation, some units had to be housed in hotels for a night or two. The security discipline was not very good, and some "umpires" complained about it later. Some officers left briefcases in open jeeps, and maps and other secret documents in mapcases that were not guarded. Key officers needed for special briefings could not be found. Before the actual invasion, some units might have to be housed in the embarkation area for as much as two weeks. Some way would have to be devised to better the security system. That much was known before Operation Tiger ever got going.

On April 24 Admiral Kirk's staff went aboard the USS *Augusta* at Plymouth. It was a foggy day, which impeded loading, and did not augur well for the operation. But what would the real D-Day be like? There was no telling. Imperfect weather was a part of the problem, just as it was likely to be part of the war.

The next day Admiral Kirk came down from London, went aboard, and his flag went up. Major General Lewis H. Brereton, commanding general of the U.S. Ninth Air Force, came aboard with his deputy, Major General Ralph Royce.

That same day Admiral Moon and his staff boarded the *Bayfield,* the Force U flagship. That afternoon the ship's boats began embarking vehicles, supplies, and troops.

The main body of the 101st Airborne Division troops (the 502nd and 506th regiments, plus supporting troops, including the 377th Parachute Field Artillery Battalion) began moving by truck and rail to Torquay. The 327th Glider Infantry men were to be moved in by sea. They arrived at Ivybridge and marched to the marshaling center assigned. No one knew they were coming, and the confusion was remarkable. The regiment was dispersed over five marshaling areas, the farthest units forty miles apart. By nightfall the regimental headquarters was completely out of touch with the troops.

The next day the task force and the observing forces sailed.

Rear Admiral Moon was actually running the exercise as he would run the big show on D-Day when Force U landed at Utah Beach. He would protect the troops and get them to Slapton Sands. "This force will firmly establish VII Corps in position north of Start Point in order (1) to ensure the capture of Okehampton with minimum delay and (2) to assist in securing a lodgement area as a base for further operations leading to capture of the Devonshire southern coast ports."

Change the name Okehampton to Utah Beach, Devonshire to Normandy, and you had a picture of the D-Day invasion.

Major General Lawton J. Collins, commander of VII Corps, would observe the proceedings, as Major General Barton's 4th Infantry Division exhibited the results of their amphibious training. He would go on the beach to get a good close look, for these were his boys who would soon enough be making the real landings in Normandy. This was their last chance to make errors without paying in blood.

From offshore, the higher authorities would watch the exercise. General Bradley and Lieutenant General Lewis H. Brereton, commander of the Ninth Air Force, would board an LCI and would watch from outside the battle zone, but close enough to see the white cottages of the village of Slapton Sands. So important was this exercise that General Eisenhower, Air Chief Marshal Tedder, and a handful of assorted high staff officers were also aboard. They wanted to see one new wrinkle devised by the airmen, the use of rockets by a squadron of British Typhoons. But what would please them most was perfect timing, and perfect execution of this exercise that so closely represented the coming battle.

8
Attack!

AT 8:21 on the morning of April 26, 1944, Operation Tiger was given an air of authenticity. German planes appeared over Plymouth and the air raid sirens began to howl. But the Germans were apparently involved only in a photographic mission, which was so common these days as to be unexceptionable, and no bombs dropped. Eighteen minutes later the all clear sounded, and the day's activities could be resumed.

At 9:30 General Barton arrived to board the *Bayfield*, and twenty minutes later the command ship slipped her mooring and moved down stream to Plymouth Sound to anchor and wait. At 3:18 that afternoon General Collins and his staff of VII Corps arrived aboard. At 5:38 P.M. the *Bayfield* was under way again, moving out of Plymouth Sound. The searched channels of the area had been extended and made complicated to simulate the difficulties the naval force would have in the real landings on the other side. The command ship was to anchor and then wait for the naval bombardment that would precede the exercise. Of course, this would be brief, and the actual bombardment on The Far Shore would be longer.

Meanwhile, the observers, umpires, and high officials were assembling in the Plymouth area to prepare to watch the exercises as they began the following day. A number of them were assigned to stay at the Palace Hotel in Paignton and others at the Sattra and Tembani hotels. That evening briefings were held at the Palace and Torbay and other hotels, to inform the watchers about what they would be seeing the next day. That night they would board various vessels at Dartmouth and spend the night afloat. The next morning the exercise would begin, and for the SHAEF and 21st Army Group crowd the affair would end with lunch at one of the hotels, whereupon they would return to London and their various headquarters.

"Exercise Tiger . . . a short movement by sea under the U.S. Navy, disembarkation with Naval and Air support at Slapton Sands, a beach assault using service ammunition, the securing of the beachhead and a rapid advance inland," said the official briefing letter from G-3, the operations division of SHAEF.

". . . During the period H-60 to H-45 minutes, fighter bombers attack inland targets on call from the 101st Airborne Division and medium bombers attack three targets along the beach. Additional targets will be bombed by both fighter bombers and medium bombers on call from ground units. Simulated missions will also be flown with the target areas marked by smoke pots."

"Naval vessels fire upon beach obstacles from H-50 to H-Hour. . . . Naval fire ceases at H-Hour."

On the voyage out that night, Admiral Moon's command ship was accompanied by *LCH 95* and *LCH 86* as she entered Tor Channel. At 10:45 P.M. they made a rendezvous with the warships USS *Barnett*, USS *Joseph P. Dickman*, and HMS *Empire Gauntlet*, and then moved along in column with the *Barnett* leading. They steamed through a U-shaped channel, heading for Lyme Bay, and the transport area, which was not quite twelve miles off Slapton Sands.

Just as it would be at Normandy, the simulated battle had already begun by the time the ships approached the shore. The paratroops were dropped at about H-4 hour, and they assembled and began marching on their objectives. The mission of the 82nd Airborne was to prevent enemy reinforcements from advancing east of the Yealm River. The 101st elements were dropped to the east, and before the troops of the main landing hit the beaches, these two divisions were moving.

The *Bayfield* went to General Quarters at 4:03 A.M. Fifteen minutes later she was anchored in 140 feet of water in Start Bay. She began lowering boats and by 5 A.M. the last of the boats was going into the water. General Collins and the staff of VII Corps went ashore just before 6 A.M. to observe from the beach.

General Eisenhower and Air Marshal Tedder, General Montgomery and Admiral Ramsay, General Bradley, and other members of the SHAEF contingent split up so that all these high officials would not be in the same boat. Eisenhower and his party were aboard *LCI 495*, right out in the front of the observers. It was a foggy day, and the wind blew spray across the bridges of the ships hard enough to wet the field glasses of the observers.

The LCIs pulled up just as the naval bombardment of the beach began. The air force had not yet arrived, the observers noted, although they were supposed to have hit the beaches first. The overcast was heavy, but that was not the reason for the failure of the planes to come in.

General Eisenhower and his party were waiting for the Typhoons to come in, and also for the effect of the DD waterproofed tanks, fitted with propellers, which were scheduled to be launched from the LCTs and make their own way ashore to lead the infantry.

The *Bayfield* was ready for the invasion of Green Beach, which was the area to be hit by the troops she carried. At 6:20 the commander of the Green Assault Group reported to Admiral Moon that some of the LCTs were behind schedule, and he recommended that H-Hour be delayed.

This action was within Admiral Moon's province, but he wanted to consult with General Collins before doing so. Since Collins had left the ship, there was no way to make the contact, so the admiral had to decide: at 6:25 he ordered H-Hour delayed for one hour.

The officers of the second wave for Green Beach did not get the message, and they landed at the appointed time. The exercise had been set up to use live ammunition and live fire from air support units, all carefully planned so that the artillery and ships would fire at times and in areas where there were no Americans. The artillery and air support had to be cancelled in the interest of safety. No Typhoons, and no rockets.

The naval firing was very accurate and was hitting targets on the beach on the hillside behind the Slapton Ley.

The LCTs with their DD tanks milled around the assembly point, waiting. The Typhoons did not come at all.

Finally the delayed H-Hour arrived, and the DDs were launched. They began moving toward the shore at about three knots. One was smoking, Captain Harry Butcher, Eisenhower's naval aide, noticed. He saw the tank move by a yellow marker buoy—and then realized it was not a marker buoy but a dinghy pushed out from the "waterproof" tank. An LCVP sped the scene, while the tank crew got into the dinghy. Then Butcher saw the tank sink. There were no casualties.

Three landing craft moved up close to shore and bombarded with rockets; their purpose was to knock out the barbed wire and other obstacles. The first landing would be made by engineer troops, whose job would be to clear the beaches of obstacles for the main force. To observers the results were spectacular, but to the experts they were ineffective. All the rockets hit short of the beach. Smoke shells fired to support the landings were accurately placed, but the wind was blowing to seaward, and this destroyed the effect of the smoke. The engineers who came up in their LCVPs were able to make the beach. The tanks crept in through the holes, and the combat engineers demolished obstacles as the high officers watched through their field glasses. This was the job the landing troops had been trained to do. Many weeks earlier Colonel Paul W. Thompson of the 6th Engineer Special Brigade had set up headquarters in one of the evacuated villages near Slapton Sands. He had begun training his men and the other engineer groups in the latest methods of demolition and booby trap management, as well as in house-to-house fighting techniques learned by troops in Africa, Sicily, and Italy.

In previous exercises, the 6th Engineer Special Brigade had been based at Paignton, near the Sands, and had practiced demolition, picking up minefields, and laying down minefields. They also practiced setting up panels to bring in supplies after the beach was secured, using all sorts of heavy equipment including bulldozers, cranes, and repair trucks, which were going to be needed to keep the beaches clear and the traffic moving after the invasion across the channel.

As these engineer troops learned, they taught others. Between January and May, all the regiments of the 29th Division, the 4th Division, and the 16th Infantry Regiment of the 1st Division, and part of the 101st Airborne (those troops that would come in by sea instead of drop) went through Colonel Thompson's survival course.

For Operation Tiger the 1st Engineer Special Brigade had drawn the lot of riding the LSTs in for the second wave operations. The 6th Engineer Special Brigade went in with the landing troops at H-Hour. In the invasion of France, of course, the early landing would be the most dangerous. (As it turned out at Slapton Sands, the reverse was true.)

The 6th Engineer Special Brigade landed on the beaches and set to work. One of the units was the 203rd Engineer Combat Battalion. Its job was to bring in LCIs, LCMs, LCTs, and the LSTs that carried the supplies for the troops. They laid out the panels as ordered when the fighting units indicated their needs; one emblem signified troops, one signified arms, another meant food and another ammunition. The ammunition was brought in the amphibious DUKWs of the port battalion.

On this day, following the foulup that had caused the delay of H-Hour, everything seemed to go wrong. The engineers on the beaches seemed to the observers to be moving very slowly. The troops and tanks were so vulnerable that the SHAEF crowd, particularly Captain Butcher, became depressed. If this was how it was going to be on D-Day, there would be a slaughter on the beaches.

One group of ten LCVP small craft did not get the message about the delay and landed elements of the 2nd Battalion of the 8th Infantry on Red Beach, so Admiral Moon withheld the naval fire support that was supposed to accompany the main landing. The result was that feeling of nakedness that Commander Butcher observed.

Some tanks of the 70th Tank Battalion landed just ahead of the first wave, and some with the wave. They went into action from the water's edge, and their fire was just about the only effective support the landing troops got.

The men of the first waves jumped ashore and began breaking down the beach defenses. The assault battalions moved inland, taking pillboxes and strong points overlooking the Ley. Soon they gained their first objective, the AA line, on the high ground that overlooked the beach.

The seawall on Red Beach had to be broken down so that tanks and other vehicles could get through to the high ground. The engineers placed two 150-pound TNT charges and fired them at ten o'clock. But the charges were not effective. The engineers had to go in and dig, and it was after 11 A.M. before the first tank was able to squeeze through the gap.

It was an exercise, and, unfortunately, it looked like one. In the early hours of D+1 there was one small note of warfare that confused many: the sound of gunfire and explosions coming from Lyme Bay behind the ships of the invasion force. It sounded as though a real engagement was taking place out there, but no one believed that. The engineers, used to the blasting of demolitions day after day, heard, wondered for a moment, and then went about their business. Operation Tiger went on, very much in the manner of all those other exercises of the past.

The later waves coming ashore walked simply up to the beach. As one observer put it; they would have been mowed down if there had been Germans up on the high ground above the beach. Once they got to the shore, men of the 3rd Battalion of the 22nd Infantry straggled along the road as if they had never learned to march. One platoon was caught by an official observer as the men sat nonchalantly on the ground four hundred yards from the "front line." The men of a mortar section set up to cover a "counterattack" were discovered sleeping alongside their weapons.

One objective of the troops was the town of Merrifield, an "enemy" strong point. The paratroops were given this objective and landed in the drop zone there but failed to "capture" the town. They called for naval fire support. The navy vessels then opened fire on the strong point, but their firing was not very accurate.

As it was supposed to be with the Germans on the other side, the 715th "enemy" division was spread thin, occupying the coastal fortifications and local reserve positions immediately inland from the American advance. The 242nd Division was the principal enemy force. When the parachute troops began falling, the 242nd reacted swiftly and in the Kingsbridge area delayed the linkup of several elements and slowed the whole operation in that area on this simulated D-Day. They held positions along the Avon River through Blackatawn and Dittisham to Broad Sands.

The exercise went on.

At 3:30 P.M. the beachhead was declared to be "secure," which it was, by the standards of the exercise.

The 916th "enemy" infantry regiment was across the Dart River, and all three battalions moved to delay the American advance. By 6 P.M. on D-Day they had begun to do so, launching their first "counterattack" by one battalion reinforced by tanks.

But the Americans beat it off, said the umpires. They were ashore and had established their beachhead. Supplies were coming in fairly well, but the traffic on the roads was jammed up. A battalion of "enemy" parachutists dropped in the area north of South Brent and began moving toward the town. That night the "enemy" 916th Infantry moved up, too, and took up defensive positions around South Brent. Elements of the 228th Division and a panzer battalion began moving toward Plymouth, and the U.S. 4th Division pursued toward the Plym River, which they were to cross on D+2.

One element of the exercise was the testing of 4th Division field intelligence work. During the exercise 126 documents were planted in the maneuver area, plus more in the hands of "enemy" troops, who might be "captured." Many of these were really German documents, captured at various places, and adjusted to fit the situation of the exercises. The point was to see how well the intelligence sections could use enemy papers to extract valuable information. At the end of the operation 96 documents were returned to the umpires.

Also, fifteen prisoners of war were planted in the exercise, ten of them German speakers, two Polish, two Italian, and one Russian. Four French-speaking soldiers played the parts of French civilians. Each of these people had some information that was important to the exercise. They were told only to divulge the information if questioned about the subject to which it applied. So Operation Tiger continued, and the troops moved steadily, if slowly, toward their objectives.

The *Bayfield* moved in closer to the beach that first afternoon and anchored eight miles off shore. General Collins returned to the ship, and all afternoon small boats moved back and forth to the shore carrying officers who came to confer with the VII Corps commander.

Meanwhile, across the English Channel at Cherbourg, E-boats of the 5th and 9th Schnellboote flotillas were preparing for a patrol run along the southwest English coast.

For months the Germans had been aware of unusual activity on the southwestern English coast. The major naval element concerned with this matter was the E-boat command under Kapitaen zur See Rudolf Peterson, Fuehrer des Schnellboote, whose headquarters was located at Wimereux, near Boulogne. The 5th Schnellboote Flotilla had already given the British something to think about. On the night of February 26, 1943, the 5th Flotilla was operating out of the Isle of Guernsey. The British convoys PW 300 and WP 300 were slated to pass one another in midchannel at about 2 A.M. The E-boats *S-65* and *S-85* attacked both convoys and sank four ships without suffering any losses themselves. Thereafter they had grown increasingly bold, and on the night of April 13, 1943, E-boats had sunk the Norwegian destroyer *Eskdale* in another convoy battle.

When the Slapton Sands training area had been opened back in January, Captain Peterson's headquarters quickly learned about the increase in activity. They missed out on Operation Beaver, the testing of the V Corps troops, but on this night of April 27–28 they were preparing to move out in force.

The Germans had intelligence from the airmen reporting Allied naval activity in Lyme Bay. The chief of the 5th Flotilla, Korvettenkapitaen Klug, had six boats ready to go across the channel. They were organized in pairs: *S-100* and *S-143, S-140* and *S-142, S-136* and *S-138.* Each of them was thirty-five meters long (over ninety feet) and carried about twenty-one men. The armament varied from 20 mm to 40 mm guns, but each boat had a pair of fixed torpedo tubes firing forward and four torpedoes aboard. All the boats could make thirty-five knots and some of them, with superchargers, could make more.

Not far away, Kapitaenleutnant Freiherr von Mirbach, chief of the 9th Schnellboote Flotilla, had also ordered three of his boats out for that night. *S-130, S-145,* and *S-150* were also going hunting in Lyme Bay.

9

The E-Boat Attack

THE PLAN for Operation Tiger called for a follow-up convoy to arrive on the scene at Slapton Sands after the initial landings on the morning of April 28. This convoy consisted of eight LSTs, the whole under the command of Commander B. J. Skahill, who was riding in *LST 515* at the head of the column.

All the LSTs in the convoy were brand new arrivals in the United Kingdom with brand-new skippers and brand-new crews. The skippers were either newly commissioned men from the ranks with a dozen or more years of service, or "ninety day wonders" with a year or so of active duty behind them. None of the LSTs had been in operation in English waters for more than a month. Five of the vessels were under Commander Skahill's normal command, but that command, LST Group 32, had never yet operated together as a group.

On the eve of the operation, just two days before sailing, Admiral Moon had called a conference of commanding officers and at the meeting had warned about possible danger during the operation from German E-boats. A British naval officer from the Plymouth command had also gone into considerable detail about E-boat tactics. The E-boats the British had been seeing around Plymouth were what the Germans called Raumboote—90-105 feet long, very fast, and carrying a small crew. They were, in fact, mostly the boats of Korvettenkapitaen Klug's 5th Flotilla and Kapitaenleutnant von Mirbach's 9th Flotilla. Officially they were called Schnellboote, which meant fast, and these boats *were* fast—thirty-five and forty knots and more with their Daimler–Benz diesel engines.

Skahill left Plymouth on the morning of April 27 with five LSTs, in the convoy called T-4, carrying mostly the troops of the 1st Engineer Special Brigade who were to participate in Operation Tiger and the equipment they would need for work on the beaches. This convoy was bringing amphibious trucks and combat engineers who would manage the landing beaches and keep traffic moving smoothly. Since their arrival from Italy, the troops had managed to beg, borrow, and scrounge a good deal of special equipment for the task, some of it not on the normal table of organization and supply for any unit. The troops scheduled for Red Beach were aboard *LST 515, LST 496, LST 511, LST 531,* and *LST 58.* The last in line, *LST 58,* was towing two pontoon causeways for use in the landing exercises so the going was very slow.

Three of the LSTs had come from Brixham, and they were scheduled to land on Green Beach, the other invasion beach of the 4th Division. They were supposed to be protected by two British escorts, the destroyer HMS *Scimitar,* and the flower-class corvette HMS *Azalea.* That was not a large escort, but the British had been at this game for a long time, and with one destroyer leading, and a corvette to chase off attackers, the protection had proved adequate in the past.

Unfortunately, earlier in the night, the *Scimitar* had been rammed by American *LCI (L) 324* while working with other ships on their way to Slapton Sands. The ramming had put a hole in the destroyer's side, twelve feet above the water line, twenty feet from the port bow, two feet long and two feet wide. When the *Scimitar* arrived at Plymouth to refuel, and the captain informed the shore, he was ordered to tie up at a buoy in the harbor. The surprised skipper of the destroyer told the shore that he was supposed to be at sea, making rendezvous with a convoy outside. No one in operations ashore at Plymouth knew anything about such a convoy. They did know that the *Scimitar* had a hole in her side and that destroyers were at a premium. When the captain told the shore that his ship was seaworthy but only if the weather did not kick up, he was ordered by the Plymouth command to stay in port and get the damage repaired. He did not send a message to Admiral Moon or to Commander Skahill, assuming that higher authority, which meant Admiral Moon and the British commander of the naval base at Plymouth, had taken care of the matter before ordering him inside. But that was not the case. Admiral Moon knew nothing of the ramming during the exercise and had no messages from the Plymouth command on the subject. The Plymouth command was busily preparing for Exercise Fabius, a British-American training operation like Operation Tiger, under the supervision of General Montgomery. Admiral Leatham, the Plymouth commander in chief, simply was not paying adequate attention to the American exercise.

Also, in spite of such exercises, the real sea war was being pursued. On the night of April 25 British destroyers had fought a night engagement with the enemy, and another attack mission was being planned for the night of April 28.

In addition, this mission, plus the two exercises, had brought an enormous increase in radio traffic to the command, and messages stacked up high. So the confusion was compounded.

Even after the *Scimitar* was taken out of service, no one thought to inform Admiral Moon, who was in charge and responsible for all aspects of Operation Tiger, including the safety of the convoy. Moon had arrived off the beach earlier and had landed the first troops on April 27 and had under the Force U protection one big transport, twenty-one LSTs, twenty-eight LCIs, sixty-five LCTs, fourteen miscellaneous craft and ninety-two landing craft. By midnight they were all empty and awaiting dawn to sail away from the beach. They waited because the commander in chief of the British base at Plymouth announced that all available escorts had been assigned to the convoys, to the assault force, and to patrols and screens.

To prevent any German interference, because Lyme Bay had often been visited by raiding forces, the British had assigned four special patrols to Operation Tiger. They involved three motor torpedo boats (like U.S. PT boats), two motor gun boats, and four destroyers. They were stationed along the line of movement of the American exercise force, from the point of departure to Portland Bill. A fifth patrol of eight motor torpedo boats was stationed off Cherbourg, a principal German E-boat base, to intercept any E-boat movement across the channel.

That night of April 27, the *Azalea* was moving along with the *Scimitar* as they approached Plymouth harbor, and the corvette's skipper, Lieutenant Commander G. C. Giddes, saw the destroyer head in toward shore. Obviously she had been ordered into port. But it was not Lieutenant Commander Giddes's responsibility to inform the convoy commander of changes in orders he knew nothing about, and, besides, he did not have any radio contact with the LSTs. No one in higher authority had dreamed there would be any need for such communication. So Admiral Moon did not know that his valuable convoy was protected by only one 16-knot escort, and Commander Skahill discovered the fact only when Lieutenant Commander Giddes showed up. First, however, the corvette came around to the area off Brixham and met the Brixham LSTs as they came out. The little convoy steered a southwest course and soon met up with the first party of LSTs under Skahill, moving along at about four knots. The line was single, about three miles long. The three Brixham LSTs joined up at the end, with *LST 507* in the tail-end position.

LST 507 was carrying the 478th Amphibian Truck Company, the 557th

Quartermaster Railhead Company, the 33rd Chemical Company, the 1st Platoon of the 440th Engineer Company, and the 3891st Quartermaster Truck company. Aboard were two ¼-ton trucks, one ¾-ton truck, thirteen 2½-ton trucks, and twenty-two amphibious DUKWs. *LST 531* carried the 462nd Amphibian Truck Company, the 3206th Quartermaster Service Company, and the same mixture of vehicles. *LST 289* carried the 478th Amphibious Truck Company, the 556th Quartermaster Railhead Company, and the 4th Medical Battalion, and the same mixture of vehicles. The other LSTs had approximately the same sort of loads.

During the night the fog came in, and soon the ships decks were dripping. It was relatively clear, however. To the British, accustomed to the channel weather, it was a fine night. The wind was light. The moon came up, and visibility was better than fair.

At 7:30 that night the convoy speeded up to six knots. It was dark and cloudy. The radar was in use to avoid small boats and locate buoys. A number of small boats were seen off to starboard, apparently engaged in towing something, but that was all, until half an hour after midnight when white and yellow flares were sighted. These had no significance to the operation, or to the combined naval forces. The Americans assumed that they were British, but, of course, they might be German. Or, they might be part of the exercise. No aircraft were sighted, but the flares kept rising. The number in the air in any given area varied from one to five. Some were rocket flares and some were parachute flares.

These flares were coming from three groups of E-boats. The boats departed from Cherbourg at 10 P.M. in two columns, traveling at thirty-six knots. They maintained radio silence, and they did not turn on their radar because they did not want the enemy to locate their positions by RDF equipment. Visibility was 15,000 yards, and the sea was calm.

Radio and radar equipment in France picked up the movement of Skahill's command, Convoy T-4, and before midnight Captain Peterson's headquarters had the information that it was out in the Lyme Bay area. The German navy had divided all the waters of the world into small grid squares marked out on special charts. Captain Peterson told his E-boat commanders that they were likely to find targets in grid square BF 2398. At that point, the E-boat formation split up to attack in smaller groups. At one minute past midnight,

S-136 and *S-138* reported back to base that they had passed two destroyers, heading west at seven knots. They fired torpedoes, and missed.

Just after midnight, HMS *Onslow*, patroling off Portland Bill, encountered one of the E-boats, but it got away to the south. The men of the *Onslow* did not even know they had been fired on. A few minutes later three groups of E-boats were plotted between ten and twenty miles south of Portland Bill, steering northwest, and searching for Allied ships.

In spite of these enemy contacts, nothing was done to protect the convoy at that time, because of the confusion that continued in the command at Plymouth.

On the evening of April 27, when the *Scimitar* was brought in for examination of the damage to her hull, the duty officer at Plymouth was under the mistaken impression that the *Scimitar* had been sent into port by Admiral Moon and that a replacement escort had been assigned to the convoy. The dockyard announced that it could not take the destroyer until the following morning, so the *Scimitar* sat at her mooring as the convoy moved on toward Slapton Sands.

At about 7:30 P.M. the British staff officer began reading the signal log and realized that something was missing. He called in the captain of the *Scimitar*. Finding the captain and bringing him to headquarters took several hours, so it was not until nearly midnight that the Plymouth headquarters was aware of what was really happening at sea. Meanwhile the E-boats were bearing into Lyme Bay.

Just before 1:30 on the morning of April 28 the Plymouth command realized what a dreadful error had been made in holding the *Scimitar* in port. The report of the sailing of three groups of E-boats that had managed to penetrate the screen off Cherbourg, meant that nine E-boats were out there somewhere, constituting a real danger into which the convoy was moving, guarded by but a single escort. HMS *Saladin* and HMS *Tanatside* were the closest vessels available to the convoy, and the *Saladin* was ordered to join up posthaste. The *Saladin* was then thirty miles away from the convoy. That meant if she could find the convoy immediately it would be a good hour and a half before she could catch up.

Lieutenant Commander P. E. King, skipper of the *Saladin*, ordered flank speed. That turned out to be twenty-three knots because the number one boiler was in bad shape and was to be used only in chasing E-boats. The course set was to intercept the convoy seventeen miles off Portland.

Almost immediately after starting toward the convoy, the bridge watch of the *Saladin* saw star shells where the convoy ought to be. Then tracer fire was observed. After that a sheet of flame rose up, and the skipper of the *Saladin* knew that some ship had been hit. Course was altered toward the burning ship. Then at 2:25 more tracer fire was seen south of the convoy, and the course was altered to go after the E-boats attacking.

Shortly after 1:30 A.M. the convoy was moving at about five knots when Commander Skahill heard gunfire and saw tracers coming from the end of the column. He was thirty-three miles from Slapton Sands. The firing lasted about a minute, and since no reports had been received of enemy vessels in the area, Skahill assumed that the firing had come from some point ashore and had nothing to do with his convoy.

Aboard the *Azalea* Lieutenant Commander Giddes also saw the tracer bullets, but *Azalea* was at the head of the column, more than a mile out in front of *LST 515*. Lieutenant Commander Giddes could see no more than the convoy commander.

The convoy went on. Half an hour later, at 2 A.M., Commander Skahill saw a ship afire off to the south, about five miles away. He looked at the escort. She was staying firmly in place up ahead. He checked the radio room for messages about a ship burning. There were none. It seemed apparent to the commander, then, that the burning ship had nothing to do with his convoy or his mission, and was just another of those strange happenings at sea that usually never were explained. Commander Skahill had a sense that something was wrong, but no more than that. He did order a constant watch on the radar.

The radar operator of *LST 515* was a busy man. Pips were showing up all around his screen. Were they "friendlies" or enemy? In these British waters there was no way to tell. And there was no way to ask the British escort vessel, which, for radio communications purposes, was completely out of touch, tuned in to channels with which the Americans were not familiar. Escort and convoy might as well have been on opposite sides of the Atlantic as far as the radio was concerned.

The convoy steamed slowly on, unaware that danger was not only lurking on her flanks, but that tragedy had already struck. The burning ship astern *was* one of Skahill's. It was *LST 507*, the last ship in the long column. She was carrying a crew of 165 officers and men and 282 U.S. Army troops of the 1st Engineer Special Brigade.

At 1:30 Lieutenant J. S. Swarts, commanding officer of *LST 507* had been on the bridge. Lieutenant (jg) J. F. Murdock, the executive officer, was in the chart house when he heard racket and stepped outside, to see a handful of tracers flying his way. Other officers reported the tracers had been firing for a minute or so and that they were apparently coming from some vessel. That was all he knew. Lieutenant Swarts ordered the ship to General Quarters, and the men manned their battle stations.

From this point on, intermittently, the men of *LST 507* saw and heard firing, but they could not identify it in the darkness.

At about 1:30 the E-boats had entered the middle of Lyme Bay. Just after 2 A.M., the *S-136* and *S-138* identified what they thought to be "a pair of destroyers." The *S-138* fired a double salvo of torpedoes at the stern of the right-hand ship, from a range of 2,000 meters. The *S-136* launched torpedoes at the second ship.

Oberleutnant zur See Stehwasser, skipper of the *S-138,* looked anxiously at his watch. Estimating the distance to the right-hand "destroyer" he had figured 95-100 seconds running time for the torpedo:

95. . . .
96. . . .
97. . . .
98. . . .
99. . . .

Then, came a most satisfying flash. Stehwasser saw a torpedo hit "in line with the second funnel." Almost at that same time Kapitaenleutnant Jurgen-meyer in the *S-136* said he saw the simultaneous detonation of both his torpedoes after they had run only forty seconds. Both E-boats then fired more torpedoes at the ships, but missed.

The men of *LST 507* felt one of those torpedoes as it slammed into the starboard side of the ship. It hit the auxiliary engine room, and immediately all electric power went out. The main engines stopped, and the ship burst into flame. The damage control parties tried to staunch the fires, but with no power the pumps would not work, and the fires were between the men and the chemical fire fighting equipment. The flames spread fast.

At 2:30 the order was given to abandon ship. Lieutenant Murdock turned over the key to the ship's office to his yeoman, so he could rush in and get the ship's records off. The leading quartermaster had the ship's notebooks, and one of the storekeepers had the whole division's personnel records.

There was no time to spare, that was apparent. The ship had not fired a gun, and it would not. The men managed to get the No. 1 and No. 2 boats over the side and filled them with escaping army and navy men. Two life rafts were launched. At 2:45 the ship had been abandoned, many men were floating in the water in life jackets, and the sea was lit eerily by the fires on the burning vessel. Executive Officer Murdock and Skipper Swarts were the last men to leave the vessel, as far as they knew.

Meanwhile, the other E-boats were chasing the convoy and preparing to fire torpedoes. *S-140* and *S-142* found the ships and opened fire, each with a double shot at only 1,400 meters. *Nothing* happened. To miss at that range seemed remarkable, until Oberleutnant zur See Goetschke of *S-140* realized that these must not be destroyers at all, but some sort of slow shallow draft cargo vessels. The torpedoes had obviously run completely beneath the targets.

And that is when the firing with the 40 mm guns began, the tracers that were seen by nearly all the LST crews, by the bridge watch of the *Azalea,* and from the shore. The two E-boats fired about sixty rounds each, and noted that they hit the ships.

The tracers also attracted *S-100* and *S-145,* which sped toward them. The German skippers saw a "tanker" burning brightly and also giving off a dense cloud of smoke that covered the bay. Through the smoke they could see random firing in all directions by various vessels. They recognized their own tracers, but also saw different colors which had to be the shooting of the enemy.

The next ship to feel the bite of the E-boats was *LST 531,* part of Commander Skahill's Plymouth section. She was right in the center of the long column when the action began.

At 1:30 the call to General Quarters sounded through *LST 531.* Ensign Douglas G. Harlander hurried to the bridge and was informed that gunfire had been seen and heard around the ship, lasting about a minute. He saw nothing, and twenty minutes later the ship was secured from General Quarters since nothing seemed to be happening.

But just after 2 A.M. the officer of the deck called on the quartermaster of the watch to log an underwater explosion. Ensign Harlander was in the chart house at the time. A minute later the three men saw flames springing up from *LST 507* in the distance, although they did not know that the fires came from part of their own convoy. Ensign Harlander and Ensign Cantrell decided that what they were seeing must be an LST in flames, and they had the impression that their convoy was under attack.

The impression became reality for the men of *LST 531* fifteen minutes later when a torpedo hit the side of their ship and a minute later was followed by another.

S-*100* and S-*145* had approached to within 1,500 meters of *LST 531.* Each E-boat had fired two torpedoes. After a run of seventy-six seconds the first torpedo hit.

It struck amidships on the starboard side. The second hit at the position of the No. 3 boat and also demolished boats No. 5 and No. 6. The LST's No. 140 mm gun began firing at something off to the starboard. The ship then burst into flame with such intensity and speed that it surprised everyone aboard. The power failed, the communications system went out, and the engines stopped. In seconds the ship was dead in the water. The damage control parties tried to stop the fires, but they had no water. An attempt was made to launch boat No. 4, but the flames prevented it.

Ensign Harlander found himself the senior officer on the bridge. The ship began to list heavily, and he gave the order to abandon. Not more than fifteen men could have heard him, there was no way he could amplify his voice. Some men had already jumped overboard. The rest that Harlander saw went into the sea, as the LST capsized and sank.

At 2:30 the *Saladin* made radar contact with an E-boat, but it was soon lost. Tracer fire was seen again in the vicinity of the convoy, and a second ship was seen to blaze up, so the *Saladin* headed toward the convoy once more. No contact was made again with the enemy. The *Saladin* plowed on to reach the convoy.

Just ahead of *LST 507* in the long column was *LST 289,* commanded by Lieutenant Harry A. Mettler. From his bridge he saw the flares going up off his starboard bow. The time was just after midnight. Then, nothing more happened until shortly after 1 A.M. when two slight jars were felt on the bridge of *LST 289,* about thirty seconds apart. The effect was similar to the effect of depth charges being fired at a distance.

At 1:30 A.M. Lieutenant Mettler saw gunfire which was apparently directed at *LST 507,* then about 600 yards astern of his ship. Lieutenant Mettler was in the super-conn, and he took over control of the ship from the officer of the deck, and the officer of the deck went to his battle station.

Lieutenant Mettler conferred with his gunnery officer, and they agreed that the gunfire was coming from 40 mm guns, 2,500 to 4,000 yards off their ship, due west. But they saw no vessels.

They saw the *LST 507* come sheering off to their port and ahead, apparently taking evasive action, nearly abeam of their ship. At the same time the gunfire from the unknown source traversed toward their ship, but most of it was high, going over the mast top, doing no apparent damage.

At that moment, the gunners were manning the 40 mm guns at bow and stern. The captain gave the order to go to General Quarters.

Again, there was no way of firing back against an unseen enemy. There were not even any gun flashes to mark the source. To fire would only be to give away the position of the ship, so the skipper ordered the guns to local control with instructions that they fire only if they could see an enemy vessel.

The firing continued for ten minutes. *LST 289* sustained no damage, but neither did its gunners ever see the enemy.

The Germans of the 9th Flotilla's three E-boats were also watching this show as they approached. They saw red tracers and assumed that these must be fired by the enemy ships, because they knew that their flotilla had been ordered to shift from red to yellow tracers and assumed that the 5th Flotilla had received the same order. Actually, this was the fire of *S-140*, which had not shifted the color of its tracer bullets.

The three 9th Flotilla E-boats then moved in to attack. *S-150* and *S-130* attacked a single LST, and *S-145* went after some small "armed escorts."

From the deck of *LST 289*, it seemed that about three hundred rounds were fired at the ship. Then the firing stopped.

After being hit, *LST 507* swung back into line seven hundred yards astern of *LST 289*, and the column of ships proceeded as it had been. At 2:03 A.M. the officers and men on the bridge of *LST 289* saw an enormous flash from *LST 507* and then flames that spread almost instantly from bow to stern. *LST 499* pulled up on the port side of *LST 58*, and *LST 289* sheered off to port.

LST 58's bridge watch saw the enormous fires start aboard *LST 507* and went to General Quarters. All the army personnel aboard were ordered to the starboard messing compartments. Some of the soldiers were sleeping in their vehicles and had to be awakened, even after all the racket.

The flash on *LST 507* was also seen by the officers and men of *LST 499*, and just afterward they also saw the wake of a torpedo abeam, about a hundred feet to starboard of the ship. The captain ordered full left rudder and all engines ahead full, the bow lookout saw the torpedo clear the ship, but not by more than twenty feet.

Aboard *LST 289* Lieutenant Mettler considered going to the assistance of *LST 507,* but he had a full complement of army passengers aboard his own vessel, and there were obviously powerful enemy units around the convoy. Given the responsibility of passengers and the ship's vulnerability, Mettler decided against trying to help.

The explosion and fire aboard *LST 507* had thrown the last half of the convoy into thorough disarray. Then, another LST, *531,* blew up, but so great was the confusion that Lieutenant Mettler and his bridge watch could not identify the vessel. Besides, they were too busy trying to take evasive action and save their ship. The LST was running at emergency speed and changing to full left rudder, then full right rudder, every five minutes. Several gun crews reported that a torpedo wake passed astern off the starboard quarter, and then another came across the port bow.

LST 58 was just behind *LST 531* when the torpedo struck her, and "she exploded," according to men of the *LST 58.* At first the bridge watch believed that *LST 58* had been hit, but when there were no flames, it soon became apparent that all the damage was to the ship ahead.

Commander Skahill became aware of the true situation at 2:18. *LST 531,* close astern of the command ship, suddenly erupted in flames. The convoy was under attack by German E-Boats, the commander decided.

The gunners of *LST 515* then began shooting and finally concentrated on the starboard side where radar indicated some craft was moving. The ships astern also began firing, to port and starboard, and the fireworks lit up the night. One of the speeding E-boats crossed the bow of the command LST, from starboard to port.

Another E-boat approached *LST 511.* First the lookouts heard the motors of these high-speed craft, which sounded much like airplane engines. Then several men saw the boat. They were S2c W. P. Waiter, SC1C R. Edralin, S1c W. L. Benson, and S2c C. Dorfman. The boat was approaching at forty knots on a course heading from port to starboard, passing directly in front of *LST 511,* not more than fifteen yards off the bow. None of the ship's guns could bear low enough to fire on it. The E-boat then made two swift turns, ninety degrees to starboard at high speed, and then it went back to its original course to port. It disappeared in the darkness.

LST 515, LST 496, and *LST 511* were all firing. The after port guns on

LST 496 swept the decks of *LST 511,* wounding a large number of naval and army personnel.

Private First Class John Behuniak of the Army 261st Medical Battalion, Company B, was hit in the left ankle; Private Mervin Sobers was hit in the ankle and the heel. Private Leo Marquez was wounded in the abdomen. Private First Class Arthur G. Olsen was hit by a 20 mm shell in the left leg.

Fourteen officers and crewmen of *LST 511* were wounded, including the executive officer, Lieutenant (jg) John W. Eddy, hit in the left eye, Lieutenant (jg) J. Yacevich, hit in the right leg, Ensign Harry C. Tremain, wounded in the right forearm and side. Wounded enlisted men from the LST were, S2c Frank Schultz, S2c Marvin Wolbach, Cox. E. H. Blazer, S2c James L. Davis, SK 2c Fred Gallagher, S1c W. J. Williams, SM3c George R. Downey, S2c Calvin M. Wolf, HA 2c William E. Fern, StM2c R. C. Sanders, and HA2c Daniel Durbin.

The other LST's gunners were trying to fire on that E-boat as it passed between the two ships, making perhaps forty knots.

One of the E-boats crossed near the *LST 58,* and at 2:25 the lookouts spotted a torpedo boat coming at them on the port bow, about 1,500 yards out. The gunnery officer shouted "commence firing," and all the LST's guns began to fire on the E-boat. The red and green tracers outlined the E-boat, and some gunners swore they had hits. But this was not confirmed. In any event, they did drive the E-boat off, for she changed course and veered outward and soon disappeared.

Commander Skahill then ordered the convoy to take evasive action, and *LST 515* began changing course every few seconds to get away from the speedy attackers. The action continued for another two hours, and the confusion was so great, that no one in the convoy really knew what was happening.

At 2:25 *LST 499* sent out a submarine attack message:

> *SSSS SSSS SSSS SSSS 3YX V 3 PQP 2800240 BT SUBMARINE ATTACK BT 2800240 K*

At the same time Commander Skahill sent out an E-boat attack message. Radio Portland, the base, acknowledged. The British warships did not acknowledge because they were not tuned to the LST frequencies.

Nevertheless, the captain of the *Azalea* saw the two LSTs explode and turned, then zigzagged, down the starboard side of the convoy. He was unable to tell from which side the LSTs had been attacked, and he was cautious about sending up starshell for fear that it would silhouette the other LSTs and bring them under enemy attack.

The convoy began to scatter. The *Azalea* was fired upon by one LST which mistook her for an E-boat. The *Azalea* then had a radar contact with another E-boat in line with two LSTs and turned, but the E-boat skidded by and was gone.

At 2:28 the gunners of *LST 289* opened up. The crews of four port 40 mm guns and three 20 mm guns saw the enemy. Some of the gun crews were firing at a slim, long, white boat that was speeding around the formation. Others were firing at a torpedo wake that was coming toward the starboard bow. It seemed to be headed at a point just forward of the stern of the ship, when it was observed from the superconn. At that moment the torpedo was just about a hundred yards off. The captain gave the order for full left rudder, but the ship was still swinging right from the previous order, and so he belayed his order, and the rudder returned to full right. The torpedo then appeared to be moving at twenty knots, and it seemed it would miss the ship.

But it struck, with a flash and a roar. The ship did not seem to be crippled, a few light bulbs broke, but no one was tossed about on deck. The starboard stern 40 mm gun tub was blown back onto the No. 5 boat davit. The entire stern section aft of the deck-house curled over, and so did the navigation bridge aft of the signal bridge. Fortunately, the torpedo had been running shallow and struck so high that the propellers were not affected, but the displacement of all that water at the screw level caused the propellers to race in the air, and this triggered the overspeed brake, which stopped the engines. They were stopped for about three minutes.

Fires started on the navigation bridge and in the crew quarters below, but the damage control parties brought forth the fire hoses from amidships, and the fires were put out before they really got going. Steward's Mate Morris Jackson picked up a burning mattress, carried it up the ladder to the upper deck, and threw it over the side. By this time the decks were slippery with fog and oil.

The commanding officer of the 478th Amphibious Truck Company suggested that the army men abandon ship. All they had to do, he said, was put down the LST's ramp, and then the DUKWs would drive off into the water and make their way to shore. That plan was considered, but as it was under consideration the word came that the flooding of the LST was under control, and that she ought to be able to make shore under power.

At 2:37 Ensign H. M. Turner, aboard *LST 58,* heard a torpedo pass by the bow of the ship, very close to the surface. Then for the next hour bright magnesium flares were sighted out at various directions. "They were apparently intended," said the captain "to keep us from making directly toward the nearest shore."

The big problem was to make headway at all with the tow behind the LST. The captain decided to cast off the pontoon causeway tow, and he gave the order. But the winch holding the cable jammed, and so it took some time to free it. Meanwhile, the magnesium flares kept bursting in the air around the vessel.

The captain decided to zigzag toward Chesil Cove, West Bay, Portland. He had to wear eastward to make it and to avoid the flares and motor noises that indicated E-boats. At 3 A.M. the tow was finally freed and cast off. At 3:02 an E-boat was sighted in the light of a bright flare about a mile and a half away. At the same time more noises were heard off the port quarter. From time to time motor noises were heard at all points from bow to stern. The tactics of the E-boats seemed to be for one boat to fire a flare, and the boat on the opposite side of the LST to then rush in to attack. The proper defense was to turn each time so that both flare and motor noises were kept astern of the LST. For an hour the LST seemed to be encircled by E-boats. But there was no attack. In fact, the E-boat attacks on the convoy were ended; the E-boats were heading back toward Cherbourg. They were sighted and engaged by HMS *Offa* and HMS *Orwell*, but they made smoke and escaped under that cover.

Later British aircraft spotted the E-boats and made several attacks. They damaged one of them. All the others were unhurt, and the nine E-boats made it safely back to their French bases.

LST 531 suffered the most casualties. No one had briefed the army enlisted men on the LST General Alarm system, although notices were posted on the bulletin board. On *LST 531* and *LST 507*, when the power failed so did the ship's loudspeaker system, so there was no way the crews could restore order.

Some of the army men thought the "abandon ship" order was all part of the exercise. One soldier leaped over the side, shouting, "Dry Run."

But some men were so unaware of the danger that they spent valuable minutes searching for their belongings. Some officers panicked and sent the men streaming into the water without any organization at all, before the abandon ship order was given. Men lost their lives, strafed by the E-boats as they came by.

Some of the life belts contained defective inflating capsules, or none at all. Some of the men had thrown their capsules away. The failure of the officers to instruct the men in proper wear of the Mae West type life jacket cost many lives. The long delay in beginning rescue work cost more.

10

After the Attack

AS THE LST convoy reformed and headed toward Portland, the Azalea took station astern, zigzagging. The captain did not go to the assistance of the flaming LSTs because as the only escort present his proper role was to remain with the convoy. He did send an urgent message to HMS *Tanatside,* asking for immediate assistance to be given the burning LSTs. He followed the convoy until the ships began anchoring in the West Bay.

At 2:56 the *Saladin* made its first radar contact with the burning ships, at 12,000 yards—two and a half miles east of the swept channel. Lieutenant Commander King decided to head northeast to try to intercept the E-boats around the point of original attack. The convoy had scattered, and he had indications that the ships were heading north. His first duty was to find and protect the unhurt ships.

When the engineers got the engines of *LST 289* started again, they discovered that the damage aft had been greater than they thought. The LST would go ahead only to port, even when backing down on the starboard engine. So Skipper Mettler had to make a wide circle of the two flaming LSTs before he could head away from them.

The ship was carrying six LCVPs to land its army troops, and five of them were found to be undamaged. These were unloaded into the sea and started up, to be used in heading the ship toward Dartmouth. By 3:15 *LST 289* was on a course for Dartmouth and safety.

Lieutenant Mettler noticed a number of flares dropped to seaward of their ship, but he saw no more sign of enemy vessels.

Actually, the E-boats were still with them. *S-145* had broken away from the others of its group and gave chase to "small armed escorts" in the area.

Those "armed escorts" must have been the LCVPs unloaded by *LST 289* to help her own propulsion.

At 3:15 HMS *Saladin* approached the position of the wrecks seen burning at the beginning of its run toward the convoy. A small object was seen in the water. When illuminated by starshell the object turned out to be the bow of an LST standing fifteen feet above the water. About fifty survivors were clinging to it. The *Saladin* closed on the wreck and took the men off.

The captain saw a number of men in the water, but he also saw several power boats moving about. The sea was flat calm, so he decided the boats would be capable of rescuing the survivors and that he would come back and check the area after dawn. In the meanwhile he would investigate the area of attack, hoping to find and deal with the E-boats.

He moved around the attack zone where the E-boats had been last reported.

At 3:15 aboard *LST 499* the radar showed several ships resuming formation and heading for the Bill of Portland. The captain ordered a course to rejoin the convoy. Just then a corvette came rushing up and crossed the LST's port bow about 2,000 yards out. More flares were seen coming from the south. The corvette then began to follow the convoy.

LST 289 moved along under her own power and that of the LCVPs; they helped her enormously in steering against the broken rudder. At 4:15 that morning one of the LCVPs nudging *LST 289* along burned out her engine, and she was abandoned. *LST 289* went on steadily, heading for Dartmouth.

S-145 was still around the area. Before she left to join the others, she spotted the derelict LCVP and put a surface-running torpedo into the abandoned vessel. When Oberleutnant zur See Schirren returned to base he reported the sinking.

There were 395 army officers and men aboard *LST 289.* They performed admirably, staying out of the way during the action, and then manning the lookout posts and 20 mm guns which had to be left by the LCVP crews so they could go over the side and steer the LST with their small boat engines.

At 4:40 A.M. when reports from Plymouth indicated that the German E-boats had been seen moving back toward their base across the channel, Lieutenant Commander King asked for permission to return to the wrecks and rescue survivors. This was granted. But at 5 A.M. he saw that *LST 515* had also returned and lowered its boats to pick up survivors. So King decided that he would be best employed screening the LST and looking about for large groups of survivors. While he was doing this, about a mile north of the first LST wreck he saw the bow of a second LST protruding from the water. He moved up to it and picked off two survivors. After taking them aboard, he sank the floating derelict with gunfire and depth charges. Lieutenant King found another section of wreckage which he believed to be a third LST's bow. It was actually another piece of wreckage, but he reported the sinking of three LSTs, and for a time confusing messages indicated that one extra LST had been sunk.

At about 5 A.M. HMS *Onslow* arrived on the scene and also began picking up survivors from the sunken LSTs. A number of other craft came up to help while Allied aircraft circled the area, trying to spot men to be rescued.

At 5 A.M. on April 28 the bridge watch of *LST 289* sighted a convoy of LCMs with a British escort steaming toward them. Fifteen minutes later by lamp signal the British patrol craft offered assistance to the stricken ship. Lieutenant Mettler refused. After all, the LST was making six knots with the help of its LCVPs.

They passed several other ships and convoys and each time refused aid.

At 5:14 *LST 499* reached West Bay and anchored there. So did three other ships. They were the *LST 496, LST 511,* and *LST 58.*

When the captain of the *Azalea* saw them anchoring he moved off to the west to search for more LSTs and pick up survivors.

At 6:25 A.M. Commander Skahill informed Admiral Moon that two ships had been torpedoed and that he was searching for survivors. This report, four hours after the event, was the first news Admiral Moon had of the attack.

HMS *Azalea* came upon the burning LSTs, but by this time HMS *Saladin* had arrived and was standing by, rescuing survivors, so *Azalea* turned with *LST 289* and began to escort her as she headed toward Dartmouth. At 7:50 the *Azalea* was joined by HMS *Brissendon,* but the *Brissendon* was informed that the main convoy was in the vicinity of West Bay.

At 9:30 A.M. *LST 289* suddenly found herself in trouble. The port screw came off and was lost. At 10 A.M. the patrol vessel *K-25* offered aid, and this time it was accepted. The *K-25* tried to take the LST in tow, but the LST's towing cable carried away. There was no other, and so the LST stood by, dead in the water, until 11:25 when a French tug came alongside and began to nudge her toward Brixham, twelve miles off to the west.

By this time the officers of the LST had counted noses. Four men of the ship's crew had been killed during the action against the E-boats, and eight men were missing. Eighteen men had been wounded. Four soldiers had also been wounded. All these were stretcher cases; the fifteen or so navy men with minor wounds were not counted. All the wounded were under treatment by Lieutenant (jg) Richardson, of the Navy Medical Corps and his corpsmen, plus the army medical personnel, who included two doctors. One of the army doctors, however, was so seasick he could do little.

Skipper Mettler had already sent word to the headquarters at Dartmouth to prepare to receive casualties. When he was ordered to put in at Brixham, he protested, for Brixham had no medical facilities. He was allowed to go direct to Dartmouth. The casualties were unloaded and shipped immediately to the 228th Station Hospital at Sherborne.

There security officers quarantined the whole hospital and swore every person to secrecy on pain of court-martial and immediate shipment back to the United States.

Having arrived safely at Chesil Cove, the commanders of LSTs *496, 511, 58,* and *499* tried to make contact with Commander Skahill in *LST 515* for instructions. But Skahill was busy rescuing survivors and the messages never reached him. At 9:45 the commanding officer of *LST 511* sent his wounded ashore by small boat to the British Naval Hospital at Portland. Then *LST 511* and the other transports sailed again at 10:30 on the morning of April 28 for the landing area at Slapton Sands and arrived there shortly after 3 P.M. The traffic control boat anchored a thousand yards off Red Beach directed the LSTs in unloading with the employment of LCTs. In the evening *LST 496* moved again and unloaded off Sugar Red Beach until one LCT damaged the port bow door while pulling away. The damage was severe enough that the door would not close, so at 9 P.M., on orders from the senior officer present, the ship ceased unloading. During the night the bow door and ramp were repaired, and on the morning of D+2 the unloading ended. The other LSTs also completed their unloading and left for Falmouth, where they moored bow and stern at Messic Point.

By this time many hours had passed since the E-Boats got in among the LSTs of the convoy. Bodies of the dead had scattered widely and drifted in from the bay toward the shore.

On the beach at Slapton Sands, unloading of troops and supplies continued from the time of the early morning landings. At about noon, Sergeant Barnett

Hoffner and his 2nd Squad of B Company of the 203rd Engineer Combat Battalion were working down on the beach when he saw a group of men standing at the water's edge, gazing intently at something. He wandered down to the beach. There, just above the tide line, lay a body, and in the water a little beyond, another. Both bodies were clad in the fatigue uniforms of American troops.

Hoffner did not even have time to conjecture, before one of the men standing on the beach turned, saw the engineers coming up curiously, and shouted:

"Christ, haven't you men ever seen a dead man before? Break it up." And the man walked away. As he went, Hoffner saw the two stars on the man's shoulders and later learned that the angry officer was Major General Clarence R. Huebner, commander of the 1st Infantry Division, and on this day one of the official observers for General Bradley's First Army. The general knew what he was talking about: only his division among all the American troops in England had been actually engaged in combat. He had seen many dead men already.

The general gave no explanations, but suddenly to the men on the beach the sounds of firing they had heard much earlier began to have a sense of reality. The war was much closer than anyone had thought.

By the time that Admiral Moon had learned of the E-boat attack and the sinking of the two vessels from Commander Skahill's belated message it was too late for him to take any effective action. The command ship *Bayfield* remained off Slapton Sands on D+1, and the admiral stayed aboard to continue carrying out his responsibility for supply of the troops ashore. But his chief of staff, Captain Tompkins, left the ship for Portland to get information about the attack. No one knew the extent of it, or whether it was part of some major enemy countermove on the eve of the invasion of The Far Shore. The sense of tension was increased that morning by two calls to General Quarters when enemy aircraft were spotted over the channel, but no attacks occurred, and eventually it became apparent that the German hornets were not aroused.

At 3 P.M. on April 28, the *Bayfield* reanchored in shallow water close inshore. Admiral Moon spent most of the day in conference. The question very much on his mind was: how much did the Germans know about Operation Tiger?

Had those E-boats simply blundered into the convoy on a general search? Had enemy agents recognized the nature of the operation as a practice landing for the invasion of Utah Beach in Normandy? And —monstrous thought —

had the enemy taken prisoners from those vessels sunk and did he now know even more?

Could the enemy now have the all-important facts as to the time and place of the invasion of France?

Captain Tompkins was trying to discover the truth of these matters in his investigation ashore. Late in the day, conscious of the dangers more than ever, the admiral issued a general order:

"E-boat attack may occur tonight. All isolated vessels will close to within 3,000 yard circle from *Bayfield* prior to 2100 [9 P.M.]. After 2130 [9:30] all movement of craft must cease and unloading will be postponed until 290600 [April 29, 6 A.M.]. Green Very star indicates an unidentified vessel is approaching anchorage. Red Very star indicates it is hostile craft. All ships will maintain alert and man half battery, and will report radar contacts of suspicious nature."

On the night of April 28, some of the questions about the E-boat attack had been answered. Lists indicated that 744 army and 282 navy personnel had been aboard *LST 507* and *LST 531* when they were sunk. The known survivors were 290. In addition, there were the dead and wounded of *LST 289,* and the wounded of *LST 511.* In the end, 749 men were buried swiftly in an improvised grave in the exercise area, and the whole affair was kept secret. The demand for secrecy came from the top, by General Eisenhower's orders, for security reasons. Concern was growing that the events off Slapton Sands in the early morning hours of April 28 would throw a monkey wrench into the machinery of the invasion of Fortress Europe.

That night of April 28, Admiral Moon informed General Collins that the unloading of all vessels involved in Exercise Tiger would be completed, except for one ship, by noon on April 29 and that he proposed sailing the naval forces out of these unprotected waters to avoid E-boat hazards.

Force U spent a restless night off that unprotected beach, and several alerts were called before dawn, but there were no attacks on the night of April 28. Next morning, shortly after 9 A.M., the shore assault leader, Captain M. T. Richardson, came aboard the flagship for a conference. Just after noon Admiral Moon signaled the shore that the naval participation in Operation Tiger had been completed. The troops were ashore, the landings had been a "success," and the navy's role was ended. At 1 P.M. the crew of the *Bayfield* began to prepare for sea. Twenty minutes later the ship was moving out through the swept channel to Plymouth Sound, where she anchored at 5 P.M.

Admiral Moon then left the ship, bound for a conference with Admiral Kirk, Admiral Wilkes, and Admiral Struble. The subject was to be the attack on the LSTs. The *Bayfield* moved up the Tamar River to Buoy No. 8 and moored. The officers of the staff of Force U dispersed. For them Operation Tiger was history.

By the time the German E-boats pulled inside the harbor at Cherbourg and moved to their moorings, the sun was trying its best to peek through the clouds. The captains of the six boats of the 9th Schnellboote Flotilla reported to Oberleutnant zur See Rabe, who had led their portion of the mission. The reports went to Kapitaenleutnant Freiherr von Mirbach, flotilla chief, and he claimed for *S-150* and *S-130* one of the LSTs, and a second for *S-150* by itself. He also gave credit to the *S-145* for the sinking of a 200-ton landing craft. In his letter to Captain Peterson, von Mirbach said this operation was the most successful of his flotilla to that date.

11

Assessment

ON APRIL 28 and April 29 amphibious Exercise Tiger continued. On the 28th, D+1, the 4th Division advanced to its D+1 objectives. The 101st Airborne troops continued their operations to the west and made contact with the 82nd Airborne Division troops, who landed on D+1 and also secured their objectives. On D+2 the 4th Division continued its attack. Reinforcements went up to the 82nd Airborne Division. The Ninth Air Force ground parties landed and established an advance emergency landing strip. It all ended on D+3, and the Slapton Sands range area was cleared.

Immediately after Exercise Tiger was completed, General J. Lawton Collins, commander of VII Corps, called for an assessment of the exercise. No particular attention was paid here to the real casualties sustained in the practice battle. Vital business was near at hand: the actual invasion of Hitler's Fortress Europe. In war lives are lost, sometimes apparently meaninglessly, and the disaster of Lyme Bay had the earmarks of such an affair, comparable, one might say, to the costly effort to cross the Rapido River in Italy, or the enormous explosion that rent Pearl Harbor in the spring of 1942 when an ammunition ship suddenly exploded. In the heat of war authority simply cannot do more than take cognizance of such events. The E-boat attack was only a part of what would have to be expected on the real D-Day, when the Allied troops crossed to The Far Shore, a shore that bristled with enemy troops and defense bastions, which were guarded by E-boats and other vessels and was protected in the air by the Luftwaffe. What had happened at sea was entirely the responsibility of the American and British navies, and, if anything, it could serve as an excellent lesson to them about what might happen in their coming responsibility to protect the invasion forces as they approached and reached the Normandy beaches.

Certainly one thing stood out in the minds of nearly all high officers who had witnessed parts of Operation Tiger: the exercise could only be called a success by the most liberal interpretation. If the landings in Normandy went like this, the casualties could be enormous, and General Eisenhower's underlying fear might be realized: the whole operation might fail.

General Bradley had already announced his concern for the future on the basis of the engineers' performance on Slapton Sands and had asked General Collins to assign a new beach commander to the engineers. On the basis of what he had seen, the command function was not properly exercised. But, of course, what General Bradley did not at the moment know was that the organization decimated in the attack by the E-boats was the 1st Engineer Special Brigade, whose job on the real invasion of Normandy was to keep the activity on the beaches moving. One unit, the 3206th Quartermaster Company, was almost completely wiped out.

As for the conduct of the exercise, the first critique was assembled by the senior officers of General Bradley's United States First Army who had watched Operation Tiger from various vantage points.

Many of the difficulties had been set up by errors a week or two before the exercise. Take the matter of maps: the infantry units could not be expected to move very well without knowing where they were going. The same had to be true of other combat units. The chief engineer of American forces in Europe had announced proudly before the exercise that all maps had been distributed to all units. But to whom? In fact, far from "all" the maps had reached their proper destinations. The correct procedure would be to distribute maps to the senior command of any unit, but in some cases enlisted men received and signed for maps that were never seen again. What they did with them is not known; probably they met the fate of a handful of "extras" given a newspaper delivery boy who is too busy to deliver them. Many of the maps never appeared on the battlefield, and various units went into battle mapless— scarcely the best way.

The naval invasion fleet was far too close inshore and motionless from first light onward. LCTs carrying amphibious tanks were prominently visible when they started in from two miles offshore. This enormous mass of ships and small craft so close in by the shore presented a ridiculously easy target for coast defense guns or mobile field batteries, of which the Germans were known to have plenty. When the real thing came, H-Hour was to be much later, not until forty-four minutes after first light, because of the problem of the tides. General Bradley and his staff feared that if ships and craft could be visible from the shore at Normandy as they had been in Exercise Tiger, assault units would suffer heavy casualties before they ever hit the beach.

The postponement of H-Hour during the exercise had upset the whole timetable, particularly that of the air forces. The landing was postponed because some of the navy's support ships were not yet in position, and Admiral Moon was unable to get in touch with General Collins, because the latter had gone ashore. That situation, of course, represented a major difference between an exercise and an invasion. When D-Day came, General Collins would most certainly be aboard the command vessel, easily available for consultation. But the fact was that Admiral Moon had made a serious error in postponing the operation. The proof of it was that as always happened "some s.o.b.s didn't get the word." In fact, a number of people and units did not get the word, and some landings were made at the old H-Hour. If that were to happen in Normandy, the result would be murderous, and the whole plan might go askew.

The confusion in the opening of Operation Tiger was apparent. Some units waited at the line of departure for two hours. Since this line was only 3,000 yards offshore and crowded with scores of small craft, it would have given a field day to the enemy artillery.

The confusion was even worse than it seemed in the line. Some units got the word of the change, and some did not. One small unit of engineers went into land at the old H-Hour and was supported by most of the rocket ships. Therefore, there was no real support for the major force when it came in an hour later. The rocket-bearing LCTs opened fire so far from the beach that only two or three of all the rockets fired came anywhere near the sand. All the rest landed out in the sea, as far as three hundred yards from the water's edge. From the sea side, the rocket fire looked impressive, but there were not going to be any Germans three hundred yards out past the beach on D-Day.

The confusion completely bollixed up the order of landing, and the engineers bogged down in moving vehicles onto the shore and above the beach. They were supposed first to clear the beaches of obstacles for the tanks, then make a roadway to get them above the beach. But the tanks arrived before the engineers and jammed up while they waited. Then along came trucks to add to the problem.

The navy LCVPs and other personnel carriers got their signals mixed and crossed the infantry battalions before they landed on the beaches. They might have crossed back to put the men in the right places, or the officers might have changed the missions. Neither was done. Instead, the regimental commander tried to cross the battalions back to their proper beaches *after* landing. Moving parallel to the beach, they were wide open for attack and had this been Normandy the regiment's casualties would have hurt the whole effort badly. What General Bradley wanted, in case of the confusion that always occurred somewhere during battle, was for the officers to alter their plans to meet the situation they faced in reality. If the navy landed the whole regiment in the wrong place, then the regimental commander had to fight his way forward and worry about readjusting the position later on in the battle. Anything less could be suicidal.

Admiral Moon had wanted to test the effectiveness of LCTs in bringing supplies to the beach in the first hours of the operation. This had been done, and the idea had been a flop. As General Bradley knew from Sicily days, there was no substitute for the DUKW, the amphibious truck, to take supplies from ship to shore in the first phase of a landing. The DUKW could waddle on up the beach and beyond. The LCT had to stop at the water's edge, which meant the supplies had to be transferred to another vehicle or dumped on the beach—and all this almost certainly under enemy fire.

And, if LCTs were ever to be used in the early phases, they had to be used better than they had been in Exercise Tiger, for the communication between LCT crews and the engineers ashore was execrable. The LCT crews apparently could not understand the signals. The generals saw some LCT skippers completely disregard the signals and decide for themselves where they would land. Several of them landed, put their vehicles ashore, and the vehicles immediately foundered in high water or loose sand. Other LCT skippers, seeing the difficulty they had got themselves into, backed off and tried another point. All very well for an exercise, but one had to assume that much of the beach area would be covered by obstacles and mines. Enemy gunners, had they been in place, would have blasted some of these vessels out of the water. Those careless LCT captains would have been blown to smithereens and so would their passengers and weapons. That is how it would be unless these young men learned their lesson before they crossed the channel.

From the army point of view the naval fire support was a dismal display. One new cruiser and one old one participated in the action, along with seven destroyers. The volume of fire seemed to the soldiers to be unimpressive. It began well enough at 6:50 that first morning, but during the final approach of the initial waves to the beach, the firing was only sporadic. What the army did not know was that the difficulty went back to Admiral Moon's decision to postpone H-Hour for an hour. Consequently, the confusion began with units getting on the beach when they should not be there, and the navy support ships, sensing what was happening, did not deliver the fire that they would be delivering if it had been a real invasion, lest they accidentally cause some casualties to American troops.

Nor did the air show ever come off. The British were to exhibit some new air-to-ground rocket techniques, and the fighters were to make some passes on the beach. But again, because of the lateness of H-hour, the air support activity had to be called off in the interest of the safety of the troops.

Once the soldiers got going, the exercise took on a little better appearance. The assault craft came in well, with proper distance between the waves. But the gunships, which were supposed to deliver fire to the beaches as the troops came up, did not perform for some reason.

Then, in came the LCIs, carrying the troops. The unloading was anything but satisfactory. Unit commanders did not control their men, and soldiers began wandering around the beachhead. Under fire not many of them would have wandered very far before they became casualties. The whole landing procedure was sloppy; an LCI was designed to discharge men and equipment in a hurry. The life expectancy of an LCI on a beach depended on the length of time it had to remain in a defenseless position, far too long on the Slapton Sands beaches.

Above all, one of the critical factors was a certain lackadaisical air of the landing soldiers as they came in, almost like bathers choosing their approach for comfort. Men in the assault craft carried bedrolls which they dropped on the beach, leaving one member of the assault section to guard the rolls. As General Bradley pointed out after the exercise, next time it was going to be the real thing. The officers and men had better realize ". . . in the actual assault, whatever shortcuts can be made must be effected so that the infantry can move across the beach rapidly and in a minimum of time, and free the beach of small arms fire. Every man who goes ashore in the initial waves occupies valuable boat space. He must be moved to the fullest advantage."

Infantrymen in assault lines could not have the luxury of carrying supplies in with them. Infantry officers could not have the luxury of someone carrying their supplies in *for* them. Some men had even come ashore carrying barracks bags. Bradley again:

". . . barracks bags were in great predominance throughout the exercise, on the beach, in the woods behind the beach, on vehicles, everywhere. It appeared more consideration was given to bringing in these barracks bags, officers' bedding rolls, and similar unnecessary paraphernalia than was given to bringing in the more necessary tools."

Certainly, said Bradley, this was going to be put right before the invasion. Men could not be left in the passive roll of guarding barracks bags and bedrolls. He had noted that all the infantry were overloaded. Changes would be made.

And, the later waves of troops that landed did so without knowing where they were going after they hit the beach. In combat, the first waves would establish the positions, and the later waves would have to be directed to the points that needed reinforcement. No recognition of this reality existed on the beaches at Slapton Sands, and there were no beach guides to tell the men where they were to go to help out.

The general and his staff expressed a good deal of concern over the arrival of the amphibious tanks. They had come in very late, in full light of day, from only 3,000 yards out. For the real thing, Bradley wanted to see them embarked on their voyage to shore from 7,000 yards out, and under cover of darkness, with their route and speed so fixed as to put them on the beach with the leading assault units. Bradley was also concerned because once the tanks hit the beach several of them were slow in getting ready for action, and several others sank on the beach edge as they tried to move in the water parallel to the beach. He wanted those tanks in quick, firing as soon as they hit the shore, and working their way rapidly across the beaches, not up and down them.

Once the assault waves hit and began working their way across the beaches, and then moved up onto the shore, the most important task on the beach was traffic direction and expedition, and it was here that Bradley was upset about the second phase. At H+2 it was essential that the equipment and supplies be moved fast. At about this time the Germans could be expected to be pulling themselves together and preparing to launch counterattacks. What First Army's observers had seen was confusion on the beaches. Too many men, with too little direction, were involved. Also, the observers had found a shortage of company officers and very little leadership among the ones who appeared.

They were piqued by the behavior of the engineers, too. One observer found a large number of them sleeping on the beach. They had not dug foxholes nor had they dispersed. At one point, some thirty officers of the 1st Engineer Special Brigade walked into the entrance of General Barton's 4th Division command post, without any semblance of formation or discipline. What they were doing all bunched up no one knew.

The problem at Slapton Sands was organization—or lack of it. That's how it was seen by First Army headquarters. Men wandered about, doing nothing in particular. They did not do what was necessary; for example, the Navy Signal Station on the right flank of Red Beach was visited by First Army observers on H+3, and they found that *not one single message had been sent.* Had this been the real invasion the ships standing off the beaches would have had no intimation of what was happening ashore in terms of unloading and supply need. That would mean disaster, if, for example, the need up front was for antitank guns to repel a tank attack, and no message came through.

One of the major responsibilities of the beach engineers had to be the direction and control of traffic. Eager to make a good showing, the administrators and staffs hurried ashore, before the infantry and chemical combat units, in some cases. That same eagerness probably would not be shown on the real D-Day, but the Engineer Special Brigade also fell down. They had allowed the beaches and roads to fill with officers and observers, wandering around, while combat vehicles were bogged down behind the mess.

"The play of the exercise," said General Bradley, "gave one the impression of large numbers of men wandering about the beach and beachhead without a specific job to do . . . any man on the beach during the early part of D-Day must be fully justified. His presence exposes him to a large volume of enemy shelling and bombing. . . . Each man who goes ashore must be a vital member of the team . . . if he is not needed at this time, he must not be brought in."

The engineers had the authority to move anybody off the roads and beaches, and combat movement had to have first priority, without question. If, during the coming invasion, the beaches filled up with high officers on tour, or public relations jeeps full of correspondents and photographers at the expense of mortar teams and bazookas, the result could be fatal.

Bradley and his staff were pleased to see that in spite of the difficulties, the engineers did get two of the Treadway bridges erected. The causeway earmarked for the Ley never arrived, of course, two essential parts having been jettisoned by *LST 58* during the E-boat attack. An invasion beach was like a city unfamiliar to the drivers of the vehicles involved. They had to be instructed as to where to go. And in this, the beachmasters failed miserably on simulated D-Day. By 4:15 in the afternoon, the First Army observer noted, there were no signs marking the beach exits, the way to the various dumps, command posts, and other installations. The Military Police, who were the traffic cops, had very little idea of what was to be found off the beaches. How, then, could they instruct anyone else?

The difficulty continued on D+1. Command Posts were designated, but this was usually done by the headquarters personnel. Directional signs did not go up. Dump areas still were not marked, nor were motor pool and assembly areas. One of the important features of the hours after invasion had to be the de-waterproofing of vehicles, to get the debris off them so they would not bog down. These de-waterproofing areas were set up inland, but no vehicle driver would have known it by reading the traffic signs.

As General Eisenhower had said from the beginning of SHAEF's existence, nobody was going to stop the Allies from landing on the French beaches. The only question was whether the Allies could gain a foothold fast enough to hang on. And if they were to establish the beachheads, then the secret was speed in movement of troops and supply. In Operation Tiger, the movement of supply from ship to beach was agonizingly slow. At 10 A.M. on D+1 only 700 tons of supply had been brought ashore, an appallingly small amount.

One reason for the slowness of supply was the priority movement of vehicles (many of them joyriders, as noted,) at the expense of tonnage. Another was the improper employment of the amphibious landing craft. They should have been worked to death. One lesson learned at Salerno, and much earlier in the Pacific, was the importance of the use of amphibious vehicles to bring up artillery, antitank guns, and ammunition to the front line in that critical period when the infantry discovered what they were really up against, immediately after the landings. This was not done; the DUKWs were not even started until late in the afternoon of D+1. (Of course, one reason for this, still unknown to General Bradley and the other observers, was the disaster to Convoy T-4, which was carrying scores of DUKWs.)

And when the vehicles brought in the tonnage, instead of bringing the material to a proper dump with like materials, the vehicles dumped it anywhere. That meant other vehicles had to stop and pick up the supplies and take them to the proper dump. Under fire on the invasion beach this would mean many casualties and more confusion.

On this beach that had been made to resemble Utah Beach the men soon saw many trucks stalled in the soft sand. The provision by the engineers for towing was totally inadequate. Tanks and half-tracks were employed to move the trucks out of the way, thus diminishing the combat efficiency of the units involved. On The Far Shore that, too, could be fatal.

Perhaps, some officers granted, the difficulties arose mainly because the men knew that Tiger was "just an exercise"; if so, then some officers needed kicking; the dismal fact was that the beaches were virtually unprotected against aircraft attack, and not because the weapons were missing. For example, the .50 caliber machine guns arrived an hour and a half late (H+135). Then, the gunners set up their guns and immediately moved off to comfortable spots and took naps. Meanwhile, as a First Army observer noted, "the concentration of craft off the beaches, as well as vehicles, tanks and personnel on the beaches presented a strafer's paradise. Tanks in the hull down position on the beach were fairly secure against observed artillery fire, but would certainly have been an invitation to Me-109s."

In the Italian invasions, 40 mm antiaircraft guns had been put into action twenty minutes after the first wave hit the beaches. The invaders had to assume that the enemy was going to make maximum use of his shock and firepower, and certainly strafing aircraft provided a large part of this effect. The Luftwaffe could not be ignored on the real D-Day.

As for the attack itself, it was most disappointing to General Bradley, "more like a peacetime maneuver than a dress rehearsal of an assault against the continent."

In essence, the invasion force scheduled to hit Utah Beach did not show itself capable of performing in a way to guarantee success. Once the troops got past the beach, they stuck to the roads. Everyone should have known that the enemy would have those roads covered by machine guns, mortars, and tanks. They had to expect that intersections would be zeroed in by artillery. In combat they were not going to have the luxury of the roadstead; more likely they would be crawling up the ditches beside the roads.

Bradley's observers were distressed by the lack of aggressiveness shown by junior officers, a matter which he discussed with Eisenhower and which so bothered the supreme commander that he wrote General Marshall about it. The problem, of course, was that at this stage of the war, there was so little to be done to make real soldiers out of half-officers. A lot of officers and men were going to die because of it. One observer, watching junior officers, remarked that the 3rd Battalion of the 22nd Infantry straggled along a road into battle in a manner that showed they did not know how to march. Nor had they indicated any sign of knowledge of battle discipline. These were troops scheduled to storm the French beaches in six weeks! In such a few days this knowledge or the lack of it could mean the difference between life and death. Once an infantryman was committed to the battle, his survival was linked to that of his squad, platoon, company, and battalion in that order. Only infantry was going to cross the beach and capture the key points that had to be taken to secure the beach and begin the drive inland. There was no place on the beach or beyond for stragglers. A lost man was worse than a dead man because at some time someone would have to waste time and energy taking care of him. The job of company officers was to push stragglers into their own lines and assimilate them immediately. Every man had to be made a fighting unit of a team. There was little sign at Slapton Sands that the junior officers were aware of this.

And what did the observers observe with the 3rd Battalion of the 22nd Infantry that day?

One platoon was encountered sitting on the ground, 400 yards from the "front line" near the Torcross exit. Their platoon commander was trying to make contact with the units to the left and the right. Apparently he was doing it all by himself because virtually nothing was happening. And the men sat, hors de combat. If it had been Normandy, a half dozen well-placed shells from an 88 might have wiped out one platoon.

As the mock attack progressed, certain postulates had to be made. One was that the surprised defenders would rally and stage counterattacks. One intelligent battalion commander had so figured and had set up his mortars to cover the area. But the mortar crews were not taking things seriously and had gone down for a nap without leaving a single man on the alert. It was easy to say: "but this is only an exercise" (the standard excuse of all criticized). "In combat the men will behave differently." Would they? Not if they did not know how.

Perhaps a meadowlark would be singing and crickets chirping in the rural French countryside, the morning warm and so quiet that the men could hear the cows chewing their cuds.

But if right behind a haystack a German infantry platoon with fixed bayonets and three machine guns was getting ready to move, could anyone guarantee that the mortar platoon was not going to be asleep on the job?

The observers, moving about in the lines, stopped to ask men questions. What were they doing? Where were they going? Why?

Very few of them knew very much. For one thing, most did not know how they were to get ammunition as they moved along. That lack of knowledge represented a failure at every level, regimental down to platoon. Of all the essentials of combat, knowledge of the availability of firepower had to be first. The ammunition carriers had to be known to their fellows and the line of supply appreciated. There could be no failure here, if movement forward was to succeed.

One of the worst failures of Operation Tiger, in terms of the saving of lives, was the collapse of medical aid procedures. As of H+3 not a single medical casualty had been evacuated from the beach. The only medical personnel ashore were aid men attached to the engineer brigade and aid men of the naval beach party. On The Far Shore casualties had to be expected from the first moment, and provision had to be made to get them back to the ships for assistance. The LCIs and LCTs would be going back to their ships empty and were the ideal craft for medical evacuation.

Here, apparently the engineer brigade had really fouled up. As of the end of the operation the brigade surgeon "was still afloat," and the clearing station established consisted of two 2.5-ton trucks ashore and four litter jeeps. They were in the wrong place, atop a high hill where they were exposed to small

Lieutenant General Sir Frederick Morgan, who in 1943 was made Chief of Staff, Supreme Allied Commander (COSSAC). To Morgan goes the credit not only for overseeing the planning of the Normandy invasion but for ensuring that friction between British and American officers did not reach unmanageable levels. *(National Archives)*

(above) Eisenhower, Churchill, and Bradley testing American carbines. *(U.S. Army)*

(below) Dummy LCTs, such as these, were positioned on the coasts of southeastern England to confuse the Germans about the ultimate destination of the Allied invasion. *(Imperial War Museum)*

An artificial harbor, or "Mulberry," being built in a floating dock early in 1944. (*Imperial War Museum*)

(left) Field Marshal Montgomery in a picture taken after the war. *(U.S. Army)*

(below) December 29, 1943—moving day in the region around Slapton Sands, as the residents make room for the military exercises to come. *(National Archives)*

(below) Rear Admiral Don P. Moon, who commanded the naval exercises off Slapton Sands. *(National Archives)*

(above) Major General J. Lawton Collins, who was in charge of U.S. Army forces in Operation Tiger. *(U.S. Army)*

With the dawn, men in full battle dress are prepared to join invasion ships for a January 1944 exercise. *(Signal Corps)*

A landing craft unloads its cargo of men, guns, trucks, and supplies on the beach at Slapton Sands on January 22, 1944. (*Signal Corps*)

A Signal detachment sets up at Slapton Sands. *(U.S. Army)*

A U.S. Navy beach battalion taking part in invasion rehearsal in England. (National Archives)

(left) A Landing Craft Vehicle Personnel (LCVP) being lowered from the HMS *Intrepid. (U.S. Army)*

(below) At Slapton Sands, American troops move inland from the ramp of a landing craft. The Navy said it would put the troops down where their feet would touch bottom; here, the Navy did far better. *(Signal Corps)*

(above) A line of transports at anchor off Slapton Sands, with the USS *Ancon* in the foreground. *(National Archives)*

(below) *LCT 362* moves into berth towing a barrage balloon during Operation Tiger, April 1944. *(Signal Corps)*

(facing page) Ducks run through an obstacle course at the U.S. Army assault training area in Devon. (*National Archives*)

(below) Three LCTs discharge equipment on the beach at Slapton Sands. (*National Archives*)

U.S. Navy beach battalion troops pose as casualties on a soggy beach during an invasion rehearsal. (*National Archives*)

(above) A loaded LST travels toward the beach during the trial trip along the English coast. *(Signal Corps)*

(below) The USS *Caddo Parish* rescued survivors after the German attack. *(U.S. Navy)*

Captain Mather (with back to camera) takes Admiral Sir Bertram Ramsey and Rear Admiral Alan Kirk on a tour of the USS *Ancon* before turning over command. *(National Archives)*

arms fire, although a better spot existed a hundred yards away. The excuse given by the company commander was that he "had been told" to go into that area. A number of aid stations were observed, and in no case was the procedure what the army staff thought it ought to be.

Altogether, the impression gained by General Bradley and his staff was that it had been a miserable performance. The engineer problem could be corrected. The pressures that had to be applied to officers and men could be expected to better that situation. And the troops would learn under fire. Those who did not learn were unlikely to return.

Beneath all the difficulties of an untried army lay another serious problem between the services: lack of coordination between air forces and the ground forces. The Ninth Air Force had not shown up at Exercise Tiger, and it would not show up in any training operations. Only in May would General Brereton announce that he was ready to train with the troops. And by that time it was too late. The troops were in their pre-embarkation security "sausages," and there was no more time to rehearse. The next man who got his feet wet stepping ashore would be going into France, and the next call for air support would be the real thing.

General Eisenhower was going to have to wait to see the prowess of the pilots of the rocket-firing Typhoons displayed. The whole question of air support would have to be worked out on a trial and error basis in the field of battle.

As Operation Tiger ended there seemed to be a discouraging number of such loose ends. Small wonder that General Montgomery and his British commanders felt that they would have to bear the brunt of the battle. The Americans had not put on a very impressive show.

12

Remedies

THE EVALUATION of Exercise Tiger made by the senior officers of the United States First Army was swiftly passed along to Admiral Moon, whose Force U was supposed to get the Americans safely to Utah Beach, and to protect them there; and to General Collins, the commander of the U.S. VII Corps. The document became the basis of a hard appraisal of all the units involved. Admiral Moon and General Collins held a series of meetings with officers of the line units to try to correct the worst of the errors. The British, some of whom believed the American troops to be quite hopeless, tactfully kept silent.

Of course, the British *ought* to have kept silent in the naval sphere, for the most serious damage of all, the loss of the lives of 749 American soldiers and sailors in the E-boat attack had to be laid at the feet of the Plymouth command, which had failed to provide minimal protection for the lumbering LSTs as they moved around in Lyme Bay for the exercise. Naturally there was no guarantee that two escorts, one fore and one aft, would have kept the nine E-boats away, but the experience of the time was that the E-boats did not seek engagement with corvettes and destroyers. Convoy T-4 had been about as protected as a band of sheep led by a single shepherd through a forest teeming with wolves. The shepherd must press on to save the greater part of the flock; he could not stop to challenge the wolves as they carried off the stragglers. And so it had been with the little flower-class corvette *Azalea* that night in Lyme Bay, a single escort, with a flank speed of perhaps 17 knots with her boilers straining, against nine 40-knot E-boats.

After the event there was plenty of time to consider what might have been.

In Commander Skahill's action report on the battle, he concluded that he ought to have broken radio silence as soon as he saw the first vessel aflame, to find out if it might be one of his. At the time he had concluded that the flaming ship had nothing to do with convoy T-4, and thus much time had been lost in taking evasive action and in calling for help.

As for the loss of the LSTs, Skahill belatedly recognized that the two lost LSTs had been hastened to their fiery deaths by carrying an overabundance of fuel oil, far more than they needed for this brief training mission.

Also—something no one had thought about before the operation—there had to be some way for the American ships under convoy to communicate with the escorts. That meant a common radio circuit. Simple, but no one had considered it. That sort of problem did not exist within the national naval services. But in the cross-channel attack coming, the naval task demanded far more intimate cooperation between the Royal Navy and the U.S. Navy than did the military relations between the United States and British army commands. In the hurry of the moment neither Britons nor Americans had realized what the responsibility entailed.

In his action report, Commander Skahill had some other observations, ranging from a suggestion that rifles and pistols be issued so the crews of ships attacked by E-boats might fire back (an almost useless gesture) to the return to the old kapok life jackets, replacing the new CO 2 inflated single-belt life belt which had been adopted. After the battle, *LST 515* had cruised the scene for hours and had rescued 132 men, and picked up 45 dead. The rescuers had also seen hundreds of dead men in the water and had observed that most of them had drowned. Perhaps the old sort of life jacket would have been better. No one, however, could know from this grisly demonstration, for the fact was that the men had not been properly instructed in the care and use of the new lifesaving devices. Thus, many of the vests had been allowed to deteriorate, causing some of those deaths, and the men's improper wearing of them had caused some more. Survivors also noted that heavy army shoes had been a serious burden when they were trying to remain afloat.

Commander Skahill's self-criticism was followed by the LST commanders' complaints about higher authority. The skipper of *LST 499* noted that after the attack no orders or instructions were received by the individual ships and no rendezvous point was given as they scattered. (Ultimately, Commander Skahill bore the onus for the disaster in the navy's eyes. Of his United States Naval Academy class of 1921, with 546 graduates, 139 members achieved flag rank and many more the rank of captain. But Commander Skahill retired in 1947, as commander, although his standing in his class had been well in the first half and with even undistinguished service he could normally have expected at least to achieve the rank of captain.)

Admiral Moon would bear no such onus, for although he bore the ultimate responsibility as far as U.S. naval forces were concerned, his actions had been unexceptionable. He had assigned two escorts to the convoy, the maximum available to him. He had begun his investigation of the disaster as soon as he learned about it, but that was nearly five hours after the fact. He had sent his chief of staff, Captain Tompkins, to the scene in an LCI, along with the USS *Tide,* HMS *Dianthus,* and HMS *Primrose* from his escort screening force to find the LSTs, bring them in safely, and pick up survivors. He had requested air search from the British and had sent the word to all nearby ports to be prepared to receive survivors.

As everyone involved knew, even two escorts to protect a long line of slow-moving vessels was inadequate escort. For future—and particularly for the voyage to The Far Shore—Admiral Moon recommended "at least" four escorts, and, if the convoy was long, then the escort should be increased so that all portions were within easy reach of an escort. After all, in E-boats they were dealing with vessels capable of over forty knots.

Admiral Moon's recommendation was sensible, but also impossible to fulfill. It was true that by the spring of 1944 the German E-boat menace had been decreased enormously, but only because the British and the Americans were working at the job, which meant the use of many ships and planes. The British now had enough escorts to work their transoceanic convoys properly, but there were still too few to meet every need. American destroyers and destroyer-escorts for the most part were going to the Pacific, under an agreement with the British that the Royal Navy would take the major responsibility for naval operations in the Atlantic.

Admiral Kirk, the commander of U.S. Task Force 122, which was the American naval contingent for the Normandy invasion, had some remarks to make about the failures of Operation Tiger at sea. The naval form for dealing with any action is to stack up the reports. Primary is the report of the commander of a unit engaged in an action, in this case, Commander Skahill. To that report are attached all the subsidiary command reports; in this case, the reports of the commanders or surviving senior officers of the LSTs involved. Then the report starts up the ladder, with each superior commander submitting his own "endorsement," which consists of suggestions and his opinion of the events. Ultimately such a package reaches the highest level, in this case, Admiral Ernest J. King, the commander of the United States Fleet and Chief of Naval Operations. The total, as presented to Admiral King, gave as complete a picture of the whole chain of events as was possible, as well as the observations and recommendations of those involved.

Admiral Kirk was concerned, as well he might be, about the failure of the British and American units to establish a line of communication. Had there been such, when *LST 507* suddenly caught fire, her captain would have been in touch with Commander Skahill, and he would have been in touch with the *Azalea* in a matter of moments. Whether that would have made much difference is debatable. But had communications been such that *Azalea* and Skahill were in contact from the beginning, perhaps Skahill would have learned that only one escort was assigned, and perhaps, somehow, he could have gotten through to Admiral Moon, the one person who could do anything about that situation. Altogether, it seems very iffy; what is apparent is that communication was marked by a lack of system and by malfunction, a matter that had to be taken seriously by the highest echelons.

One maddening aspect of the affair was the fact that Plymouth base and the British anti-E-boat patrols were completely aware of what was going on, but the ships affected knew nothing until the attack began. And the patrols, which had been unable to intercept the E-boats and knew they were coming, had no way of letting the convoy know.

Altogether, as Kirk noted, the naval units had been set up for trouble in this exercise: a convoy composed almost entirely of newly commissioned ships, recently arrived in the theater of operations, and manned by crews unfamiliar with England and Royal Navy procedures, and possessed of extremely limited tactical training. The result was predictable. From the beginning the station-keeping was not good, which meant that the tail-end ships were lagging behind, and thus made themselves "tail-end Charlies" or prime picking for the predatory E-boats. Given that beginning, with inadequate escort and no way of securing information about the threatened attack, the convoy was lucky to have lost only two vessels, with a third badly battered by a torpedo and a fourth hit hard enough by small arms fire to require many replacements among the crew.

Admiral Kirk's concern was heightened by the fact that there was no time to do another exercise for further training. Operation Tiger had indicated serious deficiencies in the American command and in the combined operations command. Admiral Kirk said: "... This engagement developed deficiencies which must be corrected prior to pending events." For pending events read Normandy invasion.

Admiral Kirk sent to the Allied naval commander in chief, Admiral Sir

Bertram Ramsay, strong recommendations for more escorts in future operations and a cleanup of the E-boat bases before the invasion was launched.

The British high command had a major responsibility in the mixup that accounted for the tragedy. But beyond that, what happened in Lyme Bay showed how hard it was for two separate national naval services to achieve the sort of cooperation on a tactical level that might prevent error. At the top all was serene. At the bottom all was confusion.

Back on January 1, while preparing for the training operations, Admiral R. Leatham, the commander in chief at Plymouth, where they would be centered, had laid out his line of command:

From the time of leaving Falmouth, the port of embarkation for the exercises, the American commander involved would be in charge of his forces, including all the British vessels that formed the close escort. Leatham had so written Rear Admiral John L. Hall, Jr., who was Admiral Moon's opposite number, in charge of the landings of the V Corps at Omaha Beach. Admiral Hall had carried out Operation Duck and Operation Beaver.

"Should I have any information of enemy attack by E-boat, submarine or air, it will be passed to you to take such action as you may think fit. I regard myself as free to suggest action if necessary."

This, of course, did not happen. No word of the E-boats was passed to the Americans.

So in the beginning, the system of command had been established clearly on the high level, but, in fact, it did not function on the operational level. In the operations previous to Tiger this made no difference. The enemy did not attack, and no one noticed that if he had attacked there was no way for the American sheep to get in touch with the British shepherds.

What was also apparent, and this was noted by Admiral Leatham in his letter on the subject, was that the whole setup for the exercise was very similar to that planned for the Normandy invasion. Two escorts for the LST convoy, operational control of the escorts by Admiral Moon, but without communication, and yet no knowledge by the British forces at Plymouth that there was no communication. The LSTs should have been tuned in to the Plymouth wavelength throughout the exercise, and they should have received the signals direct as they came from Plymouth to the escort. In fact, that would have been almost completely academic, since few signals were sent and those were anything but informative.

Three of the British escort commanders were questioned about the disaster.

Admiral Moon had a talk with Lieutenant Shee of the *Scimitar,* which had been originally detailed to the LST convoy. Shee explained that when he had arrived at Plymouth, he had been hauled in for repairs by the orders of the staff officer in charge. Lieutenants did not question lieutenant commanders and above, period! So Lieutenant Shee brought his vessel inside. He had not informed Admiral Moon of the damage to his ship earlier, because he thought the damage slight, and he informed Plymouth only as a matter of routine. It was the Plymouth duty officer who had got the wind up and created the first confusion.

Nobody sent Admiral Moon any dispatches about anything.

Nor did anybody aboard the LSTs send any messages to the *Azalea* after the visual signals when the *Azalea* joined up with the convoy on the evening of April 27. Neither the British nor the Americans knew what wavelength they might share, nor did they even think of the need for it. So throughout the engagement the *Azalea* commander and the commander of the convoy, Commander Skahill, had no communication. This did not seem particularly odd to Lieutenant Commander Giddes of the *Azalea,* for he had just recently come in from ocean escort duty and knew very little about these exercises. But even in escort duty, by 1944 the communications between escort commander and escorts and the convoy itself had become far more refined than this.

Lieutenant Commander Giddes thought it quite odd that he would be sent out to escort a convoy alone, but he said nothing, for to whom was he going to say it? Admiral Moon asked if Giddes had protested. He had not. Moon did not ask to whom would he protest? As the investigations developed, it became clear that here was a major source of the problem involved: Giddes had not made any arrangements with Skahill for communications, nor Skahill with Giddes, for they had joined up after the convoy came out, and that was hardly the time for such discussion.

There had been plenty of time for such discussion a few days earlier when all concerned had met in the preoperation conference held by Admiral Moon. And nothing had been done, because events were moving so rapidly, because Operation Tiger, after all, was an exercise in home waters, and no exercise had ever been bothered by the enemy.

When the reports went up to Admiral H. R. Stark, commander of American naval forces in European waters, he saw that the British had been true to their own system, one they had developed over four years of fighting enemy attacks. Operational control of the covering forces rested in the hands of the admiral at Plymouth because such home commands had available immediately the results of shore radar search and air reconnaissance under the British system. Thus patrols and convoys were supposed to have the benefit of swift passage of information. The system fell down this time because of the new factor: the attempt at collaboration by British and American forces. Through oversight no one had set up the necessary system of communications between the British and the Americans.

The last word from the navy's point of view was Admiral Stark's:

"No further action is contemplated."

Which meant that there would be no higher level navy investigation of the disaster and no court of inquiry or court-martial.

Admirals Moon and Kirk met with Admiral Leatham, and for the coming invasion of the continent a system of communications was worked out. There was no guarantee that the E-boats and submarines would not be out on D-Day to contest the Allied invasion. Indeed, it was expected that the Germans would use everything they had. But at least the system was established so that maximum safety with the force at hand could be given the troops who would invade Utah Beach.

13

General Collins's Findings

GENERAL COLLINS, who would be directly responsible for the success or failure of the American troops on Utah Beach on D-Day, saw that many changes must be made in operational procedure if the attack against the Germans was to succeed.

He was generally pleased with the early naval fire support of the troops that landed on Slapton Sands. But the rocket attack by the rocket ships was a dismal failure. And he recalled that his forces had been thrown into confusion by the hour-long delay of H-Hour and did not receive the naval gun support they had expected when they hit the beach.

All this was brought out at a series of briefings, the last involving various other elements of the SHAEF command.

Admiral Moon attended the VII Corps briefing and gave some responses. A number of his answers related to questions that had been raised. He had told all his officers to look out for E-Boats, he said, but the E-Boats had gotten in anyhow. They might have to face that same problem on the real D-Day.

He passed along an important lesson with regard to the life belts. Anyone who wore his life belt too far down, like a belt, found that it threw him face down in the water. That had caused many casualties, and the troops would now be taught to put on the life belts in the proper way.

One of the reasons the unloading on the beaches had been slow was the shortage of LSTs during the operation. The shortage was real and theater wide and was now augmented by the loss of the three LSTs sunk or put out of action in Operation Tiger. General Eisenhower had asked the Joint Chiefs of Staff in Washington to provide more LSTs. On the beaches at Slapton Sands, they had used British vessels with which Americans were unfamiliar to carry cargo. This had slowed down the unloading. Also, the level of training of the navy beach parties was not what it should have been. Their training would be continued right up until the invasion. "We are going to have a plan that will work," promised the admiral.

The revised plan would not be without its special risks. The LST shortage meant that instead of carrying 185 men the LSTs were going to have to do what no one wanted to do: carry 400 to 500 men.

Someone from General Collins's staff asked worriedly if the navy was going to land the men "where they wanted to be landed" and when they should be landed, a question posed by the false start of Operation Tiger.

"In every landing some units have not landed where they expected," said Admiral Moon. "You must face the possibility that that will occur and get it corrected the best way it can be. But you asked if you are going to be landed where you want to be landed. It is a navy job and we propose to do it."

Questioned about the decision to delay the H-Hour of Operation Tiger, the admiral was totally frank. "I made a poor decision," he said. "I learned a great deal by this delay in H-Hour. The lessons:

"Air does not have sufficient gasoline to take a delay of more than 45 minutes. [That is why there was no air support.] Another thing, we have a juggernaut. . . ."

Indeed, they did. Once action began on D-Day, the navy's Operation Neptune, the task of delivering the men to the beach, would flow right into Operation Overlord, the attack on the Normandy shore. By the time the ships were approaching the land, the airborne troops would already have dropped, and the Allies would be committed to the action. There was no way any person could stop the chain of events at that point.

The admiral pointed out several matters that would be especially important on the real D-Day: the probable slope of the beaches would be greater than it was at Slapton Sands, and it might be impossible to land the LCTs at all when the tide fell too low. They had used every available craft in the Slapton Sands exercise, and they still did not have enough. The loss of two LSTs and the disabling of another had reduced the reserves to zero. They had to have more for the real thing and they would get them somehow.

The meeting broke up with some halfhearted mutual congratulations. Altogether, said Admiral Moon, Operation Tiger was "a fine job," a remarkable performance with 200 craft arriving at scheduled times in the assault area.

It seems doubtful if anyone attending was much impressed by that statement, in view of the known facts. But one thing certainly was established. Something had to be done to improve the communications setup all around. That was a salient lesson of the failures.

They would have to expect enemy attempts to jam radio frequencies, and they could not count on radio communication being effective during the assault period. During this practice, the navy ship and shore parties had tried to use carrier pigeons. But that system did not work; the pigeons became confused and did not perform. Messages would have to be visual or personal, until the ship and shore system could be established. The admiral and General Collins had talked over these matters and they were agreed.

General Collins was not as upset about the ragged performance of the landings as were some others:

> The LCGs [gunships], LCTs with some tanks and the rocket ships were late in getting into position and the decision was made to postpone the landing one hour. This will not be done in actual combat. Unfortunately with the lack of communications, one group of small craft actually landed on Red Beach and put them ashore about on time.

They had, indeed, hit the beach at 7:30, ten LCVPs carrying much of the 2nd Battalion of the 8th Infantry Regiment. The troops did a fine job, the observers said, leaving the landing craft rapidly and starting to break down the beach defenses.

> Therefore Admiral Moon decided not to fire Naval Support. Don't judge the volume that we had in this exercise as what we will have for the real thing. The volume of fire will be greater and the fire will come down on approximately 4,000 yards of the beach. The fire will continue until the landing wave is 1,000 yards from shore. It will then shift to the flanks and will continue to shoot to the flanks. The LCGs [gunships] and LCRs [rocket ships] will come along on the flanks of the landing waves and will take up the fire. I was assured yesterday that they will come in and will continue to fire right out front of the two leading battalions until they hit the beach. The big rocket ships did not fire. The only ones that fired were the light ones. That picture was different also. I am confident the admiral will get them there in time. That is the picture of naval support we will get. Air support will come at the same time.

When the landings began —after the hour delay—the observers saw the men coming onto Red and Green beaches on schedule, without the air bombardment or the protection of the naval guns. Tanks of the 70th Tank Battalion landed just ahead of the first wave. They went into action at the water's edge. Their fire, the observers judged, was most effective in giving protection to the troops on the beach at a crucial moment. When the later waves came in, the men apparently were not as keyed up for the exercise as the early waves had been. The observers saw too many men standing up and walking slowly. If that happened on the real D-Day there would be heavy casualties. But, as everyone knew, the presence of some shellfire coming the wrong way was a great leveler. Undoubtedly, when their lives were on the line, these men would get down quick.

Generally, the observers said they were pleased with the way the assault battalion moved against the pillboxes and strong points overlooking the Ley. "These operations were vigorously carried out and the assault battalions rapidly gained the AA [first] line on the high ground overlooking the beach."

One aspect of the operation that troubled General Collins as much as it did General Bradley was air support. Only recently had General Eisenhower managed to secure control of the air forces during the Normandy battle. The Ninth Air Force had been established to assist in tactical support of the army forces, but the coordination of ground and air fighters was far from perfected. The army could not expect too much, but there was much to be expected. For Operation Tiger, the "defenders" had built up a point called Merrifield in the manner of a German defense stronghold. It had been hit by naval gunfire and then plastered by bombers, but the assault on Merrifield had not been as successful as General Collins's observers could have wished. The army troops did not make proper use of navy-controlled fire, which could have been directed down on Merrifield in the initial assault phase. Thus they had to use army artillery and mortar fire extensively. If they had used the navy's resources more fully, they would have saved ammunition and cut down the problem of resupply on the beaches in the initial phase of the assault. The observers were not particularly happy, either, with the result of air force bombing of the Merrifield area. To this, General Collins had a different approach. As he put it:

> It is by no means expected that the Air Corps will knock out batteries, but this fire by Air Corps is on call from the 101st Airborne unit, which is going to attack this place. This unit must be there and coordination must be timed to take advantage of it. It is not expected that the Air Corps can take out batteries by bombing. The attack must be made in conjunction with the ground troops. In my opinion the bombing was excellent and if the troops are ready to follow, they will get a great deal of help.

He had been talking to General Bradley about air cover, and Bradley had spoken of his experiences in Africa and Sicily with enthusiastic support for the airmen. So Collins was convinced that he could count on bombing and strafing to ease the job of the troops.

In Operation Tiger, the smoke that had been called for had gotten in the way of the troops landing. So in the landings on Utah Beach there was not going to be any smoke, although General Barton would very much have liked some smoke bombs to be dropped by the airmen. Out of deference to the 4th Division commander, Collins called for a new conference on fire support, with army, navy, and air force representatives. They would work out the details before D-Day.

After the troubles of Exercise Tiger, Admiral Moon and General Collins had met and agreed that the line of departure of the invading forces would have to be much farther out from shore than it had been for the Slapton Sands operation.

Observers had watched the operations of the airborne troops, particularly in view of Air Marshal Leigh-Mallory's gloomy prediction that they would be massacred on landing. The principal "enemy" force in Operation Tiger was the 242nd Infantry Division in the Plympton–Cornwood–Holberton area. This unit reacted to the dropping of parachutists in the Kingsbridge area and put a battalion into action against them, which seriously delayed the linkup between the American parachutists and ground forces. On D+1 the enemy got some of his own parachutists into action, in the South Brent area. But on D+2 more American parachutists dropped in the area and forced the "Germans" back.

Of the 126 documents that had been planted by the umpires for the maneuver, 96 were turned in, which meant they had been discovered and used by the assaulting forces. The paratroops and the 4th Division were given credit for making good intelligence use of the documents, with an exception or two. One document was two years old, which seemed a little much to the umpires. The "plants" who spoke German, Polish, Italian, Russian, and French were told not to reveal their information unless questioned about that subject specifically. About 60 percent of the information they carried was extracted by interrogation and 25 percent of it found its way onto the situation maps. Very good results were secured from French and German interpreters on the American side; virtually none from the other languages. The Americans did not have adequate interpreters.

There were holes in the performance. Mine detection and removal by the engineers left much to be desired.

General Barton, the 4th Division commander, said:

"The methods used for mine removal would have resulted in extremely high casualties had the field actually been armed. Minefield marking was generally unsatisfactory. Smoke mines were seen set off by self-propelled artillery on the road west of the causeway, and late on the afternoon of D-Day vehicles going into bivouac areas set off numerous scattered mines. By the afternoon of D-Day a large number of mine detectors had been put out of action and no provisions for replacement or repair had been made." In combat that would never do.

General Barton said he was particularly worried about his men and mines:

> We are completely devoid of mine consciousness and a hell of a lot of us are going to be killed, and you can put that in your book.

As a test of the division's ability to react to sudden change, the scheme of maneuver was altered just before H-Hour. The division staff responded nobly, overlays of the change with new boundaries and objectives were made at the Division G-3 post and were delivered to regimental commanders on the beach. By dark the division had reached the line running along the road on the north boundary, and the units were in their proper zones, with the 22nd Infantry on the right, the 12th Infantry in the center, and the 8th Infantry on the left.

During the night of D–D+1, division issued new orders and at 6 o'clock on the morning of D+1 the troops jumped off on an attack. They moved well and were ready on the following day to attack again. The infantry troop movement was certainly one unexceptional part of the operation. At least, it almost was. Some holes were noted by General Barton.

The engineers who were supposed to blow the seawall on one beach landed 500 yards from the seawall. Before they could blow it, they had to move up all their heavy equipment, this meant traversing the beach, which on the real D-Day would be hot with gunfire.

When one battalion of the 22nd Infantry came in, the units were reversed in order and had to cross each other to get into planned position. And in the landings, some infantry stood off as told and waited to land from their LCIs until sections of Treadway bridge could be landed. In fact, the Treadway bridge was put ahead of the Reconnaissance Battalion on the schedule. That, of course, was very dangerous business.

General Barton was worried about the confusion on the beach. "Too much milling around early in the game. We must bring in only those things which are necessary for the landing and holding of the beach . . . every move must result in the proper order. Nobody must interfere with it."

Barton had also noted the confusion on the beach where the engineers were supposed to have made order. The lack of signs and the lack of organization bothered him as it had General Bradley, and, like General Bradley, he did not know that most of the trouble stemmed from the losses suffered by the 1st Engineer Special Brigade in the battle of the LSTs.

On the Normandy beach, men's lives were going to depend on how fast the communications could be set up and how well they could be maintained. At Slapton Sands there were many sloppy performances. Communications wires were set up from beach to forward areas and then chopped up by tanks and trucks. If that sort of error were made in Normandy, the failure of the wire might mean the success of an enemy counterattack at a vital moment.

Another problem that had developed just off the beach at Slapton Sands was the failure of certain self-propelled guns and tanks. Replacements were needed in a hurry, but the loading at the "hards" had been done in such a fashion that they were not readily available. Also the loss of the amphibious tractors in the two LSTs that were sunk was felt in the exercise.

The parachute troops of the 101st Airborne Division had been given the task of taking the Merrifield stronghold. They had some difficulty in getting naval support fire on that target. The plan called for air strikes, but the air strikes never showed up. Brigadier General Anthony MacAuliffe, commander of artillery for the 101st, felt that his artillery performance was below par, too. The divisional artillery did not get into action until the afternoon of D-Day. The 4.2-inch mortars never did get in position to fire on the Merrifield area, and communication with the infantry collapsed. The junior officers did not have information as to the exact location and strength of enemy positions such as pillboxes, wire, and gun locations, so they felt their way. Part of the 101st came in by ship, on D+1, and they were landed helter-skelter. Enlisted men came ashore without their officers and no one was there to tell them where to go or what to do. Officers were put ashore without knowing where their men were.

Then the troops ran into serious congestion on the roads, and they helped make the congestion worse. They bunched up on the roads, sometimes took up the entire road while marching, and during rest periods they blocked the roads by sitting or lying on both sides with feet and weapons extended nearly to the center. These, after all, were narrow English country roads, not American superhighways.

When the troops moved across country, they showed no sense of cover. They failed to take advantage of concealment afforded by hedgerows and moved across open fields. The Germans were going to be waiting for them to do that on the other side.

The seaborne units of the 101st Airborne did not assemble in their area until 6 P.M. on D+1. As for the airborne infantry, they were operating over a very wide area, and they were not properly familiarized with the plans of the 4th Division. Communication was almost entirely by radio. Wire communication was not established by 1:30 on D+1.

Communications. Not a very exotic topic but vital. During the Normandy landings they would have to have a really intricate system of communications from sea to shore. During the exercise, the *Bayfield* was not equipped to handle this complicated a system, and in fact, it was a rush job to get her ready for the exercise at all. But immediately afterward, a modern military switchboard system was installed, and General Collins expected the vessel to be completely prepared for the invasion, when it came. It had better be. Otherwise, he was going to be out of touch with his troops.

Ashore, in Normandy it was going to be vitally important to get the artillery action effective at the first moment. This had not happened at Slapton Sands. No wire lines were established between the 4th Division artillery and the 188th Field Artillery Group. Therefore, they had to rely on radio communications and these were not reliable. At one point a general "serenade" of fire was called for, and it was not delivered for forty-five minutes. Some units were not even called on to fire—the 155 mm gun battery was not called to use those big guns in support of the division artillery.

The artillerymen never did know what was going on in the battle. They had only the vaguest conception of their general mission before they went into the exercise, and after it began they got nothing.

Also, the artillerymen were woefully incautious in the movement of their vehicles and weapons. One battalion was landed far from its appointed place. The artillerymen then drove directly through the seawall and the minefields without any regard for their existence. Some of the men did not know about them. In France they would never have made it.

On the other side, they were going to have to assume that the enemy had mined anything that was not marked as cleared and act accordingly, if they wanted to live.

Another battalion went charging ashore, actually detonating smoke mines on the beach. Those smoke mines represented German mines, and so each detonation represented casualties in men and vehicles.

As for air support, there was no way of knowing what might be done until the actual invasion took place. The enemy would have the say. If he was weak, then in a matter of hours airfields could be taken and operations of the 9th Air Force fighters could begin from Normandy beaches. But if the enemy was strong and the Luftwaffe appeared in force, then the 9th Air Force would have to continue to operate from southern England. It would be a handicap, but it could be done; it had to be done if necessary. "We have got to be flexible," said General Collins, and he meant in every way.

The mission of the 82nd Airborne Division was to prevent enemy reinforcements from advancing east of the Yealm River and to protect the VII Corps southern flank west of the Erme River. This was very similar to the mission assigned the 82nd for the coming invasion—to hold off the Germans from bringing reinforcements up to the Cotentin Peninsula and prevent them from passing Ste. Mère-Eglise. In the practice exercise all went well. Contact with the 101st Airborne Division was duly made at Sequers Bridge on D+1 at 5 P.M., and thereafter the two divisions moved in concert. But the fact was that very few of the men actually dropped by parachute, so the real impact of the airborne operation was not achieved. It is one thing to simulate an airdrop with all its problems of units missing the drop zone and trying to find their way to their positions, and it is another to do it all on the ground, with simulations. The airborne operation was just too easy and too successful. The VII Corps staff was concerned because the airborne men's communication with VII Corps was inadequate. But there was communication, and reception and operation of radio networks did work. What would it be like if half or more of the radio sets were lost, and the troops were wandering around with no communication, units scattered to the winds, men attaching themselves to the first officers they could find, and officers rounding up men from any unit at all so that they could keep moving and try to reach their objectives?

That might happen, particularly to the airborne. The only indication of the danger in the exercise was on D+2, when for five hours atmospheric conditions made radio reception almost impossible. That was just a taste of the difficulties that could become real in the coming invasion of France.

A composite force of the 87th Armored Field Artillery Battalion, Company B of the 4th Cavalry Squadron, and Company C of the 746th Tank Battalion was to move across country after landing and reinforce the 82nd Airborne Division. The commanding general and the headquarters group landed at 7 P.M. on D-Day, but no other troops got ashore then, except the company from the tank battalion. The other troops came ashore on April 28 and marched across country without the tanks, which had gone on ahead and linked up with troops of the 101st Airborne. Finally, the whole unit got together at Sequers Bridge without meeting any sizeable enemy force to stop them, but it was a lucky and ragged performance. Once again, the failure of communications procedures had caused the difficulties. There was also one real blooper: an out-and-out violation of security, with respect to "secret weapons," in this case the amphibious tractors. As they landed, someone said over the radio in the clear: "Look to the left and see what is coming through." General Collins was so angry about this "breach of security" that he promised to run down the source and see that it did not happen again. "I would hate to be in the shoes of the man or officer who should disclose these highly secret matters or violate our security."

Once again, security. The concern was for the security of the pre-Normandy invasion period and was really a case of the high command's mixing apples and oranges. General Collins's remark reflected one of the reasons Operation Tiger did not succeed the way it was hoped. And that problem would not exist on the morning that the Allies landed on the French beaches.

Meanwhile, General Collins addressed himself to that overall problem and promised that there would be rehearsals of all communications procedures among army, navy, and air force officers well before the real invasion took place.

The air force role in Operation Tiger had been totally inadequate, largely because the air force was new in the picture. American airmen and foot soldiers had very little experience in working together, and they were going to have to acquire some sort of system in an enormous hurry if the air force was to be helpful in Normandy. Too little was known by one service about the other. For example, during the operation the airmen were twice requested to perform night reconnaissance flights. As Colonel Taylor of the Ninth Air Force explained, the air force did not have the capability for night reconnaissance.

As for bombing, the airmen could not bomb without satisfactory visibility. And they had to have notice: an hour for reconnaissance flights, an hour and a half for fighter bombers, and two and a half hours for medium bombers.

The airmen had discovered in this operation that they and the infantry were all mixed up about the coordinates of bomb lines. This had to be fixed and so did the failure of the pilots to pay attention to orange smoke flares sent up by the infantry to mark targets. After the first day the infantry had gotten so disgusted they stopped asking for air support.

General Barton explained the problem from the infantry viewpoint. Unless the airmen could get on the target when the infantry wanted them, the foot soldiers were better off having no air support. "Take a certain hill: you are going to make an attack in three hours. Bombing is good. Bombing . . . later is no good."

Air support could be useful, but only if it could be brought in quickly and on target. Could the airmen do that? Colonel Taylor said they could. That discussion indicated how primitive were the relations between aviators and infantrymen less than two months before the invasion.

The security problem had also interfered with the successful management of Operation Tiger. The Ninth Air Force, newly come into being and newly assigned the troop support mission, "had not been Bigoted." Since the personnel involved had not been admitted to the secrets of D-Day, they could not be given much information because Operation Tiger was a direct rehearsal for Normandy. Thus, the airmen did not know what they were supposed to do or why, and consequently they did not do much of anything.

As far as VII Corps went, the most disappointing part of the operation was the performance of the engineers on the beaches. From the beginning the unloading of the ships ran into trouble. Lack of road material at the water's edge was an unforeseen problem. Some roads had become impassable due to heavy use, and there was not much that could be done about it. There were not enough cargo nets, and so unloading was again delayed. The port personnel showed their lack of experience. The total tonnage of supplies for Operation Tiger was 2,376 tons, but only 1,390 tons were moved across the beaches during the whole operation. Colonel Caffey, the commander of the engineers, explained that the actual enemy action against the LSTs was at the root of these problems. What he did not say, of course, was that precisely the same thing might happen on D-Day. He did point out that on the night of D-Day the engineers had moved enough material to the beach dumps to resupply the 4th Division with ammunition and food. And he replied to the criticisms of General Bradley and others:

"There has been mention of some confusions on the beach. Those are to be expected. The thing is a scene of wild confusion. I can assure you that there is organization and that the Brigade is working out this confusion. If a person could come back after the necessary time, he would find that straightened out."

It was true, Caffey said, that traffic control was a problem. "There are still some people who go to traffic jams. This was just an exercise, but that sort of thing is not going to happen on the occasion. The MPs are going to do something."

As for the shortages of material, "that was caused because it did not arrive on the beach," said the colonel.

But Caffey's statements, except for the note about the battle of the LSTs, did not really answer General Bradley's complaints or concerns. The general was worried because too many of the troops and officers regarded the operation as just another training move and did not recognize or take advantage of the enormous effort that had been made to make Slapton Sands into a duplicate of the Normandy they would see in such a short time. Late in 1943 the Slapton Sands area was turned over to the Americans by the British for training purposes. Lieutenant Colonel James K. Gaynor of V Corps had been assigned along with Captain John C. H. Lee, Jr., to design an invasion rehearsal area. They first were told to make it look like any place in France. But later the orders were changed, and the invasion areas were made to look like the places where V Corps and VII Corps would actually land. General Leonard T. Gerow, the commander of V Corps, and General Collins had both spent many hours going over the ground and satisfying themselves that this was, indeed, the best rehearsal area it was possible to prepare, with the same sort of terrain and the same sort of obstacles created that they knew from intelligence would exist on the other side.

So the preparations had been made very carefully, except that in the interests of security, the troops were not really properly informed of the importance of what they were doing, so many of them lost the chance to profit from the experience.

Yet, in spite of all, from General Eisenhower's point of view, there could be light at the end of the dark tunnel of error. General Lee, the deputy theater commander, told Collins and the others assembled at the critique that he had seen great improvement in these exercises, and he congratulated them on the frankness and clarity with which they had discussed the many problems. General Collins quite properly had the last word about the future on Utah Beach.

"I haven't the slightest doubt in the world, gentlemen, we are going to make it good."

What else was he to say?

Where Are
the Bigots?

AS GENERAL Collins remarked at several stages of the recapitulation discussion after Operation Tiger, many of the errors of the officers and men were caused by the inability of the high command to communicate with those who were not privy to the major secrets of the coming invasion: where and when the Allies would land against Fortress Europe.

Only the Bigots knew those facts, and they were but a handful among the hundreds of thousands who would be in the invasion. There were some who knew part of these secrets who were involved in the exercises at Slapton Sands. These were engineers who were engaged in something new that was to be tried out in the Normandy invasion.

In Africa and Sicily and Italy the engineers had gone ashore early to make it safe to bring in the tanks. In Normandy a new wrinkle was to be tried: bringing in the troops and ammunition in amphibious tractors—DUKWs. These amphibious tractors were a new secret weapon, a development of the Pacific War, used for the first time by the marines at Tarawa. When not in operation the DUKWs in England were kept under black shrouds so that no one would discover that they were self-floating. Some of these vehicles were aboard the LSTs sunk off Slapton Sands. So there was secret enough to worry about. Other parts of the secret known to some at Slapton Sands were the sorts of guns that would be used and the manner in which they would be brought ashore to start firing; also the timing of the landings, and, of course, the place of the landing of VII Corps.

When General Bradley heard that there had been enemy action at Slapton Sands, the thought that something out of the way might have occurred did cross his mind. But he left that to the intelligence people. He was more concerned about the failures he saw on the beaches than he was about possible problems about which he knew nothing.

Immediately on learning of the attack, the British intelligence services jumped to the question: why had the Germans attacked just then, and what had really happened? When the inquiries began and the wraithlike nature of the E-boat attack was disclosed, the intelligence men became even more suspicious.

What was the purpose of this attack? Had it been to take prisoners, and, if that was the reason, had any prisoners been taken? If so, who were the prisoners and how much did they know?

If some of the prisoners were Bigots, should not SHAEF consider calling off the whole invasion? For as everyone had been warned over and over, the whole success or failure of the incursion would depend on the Allied ability to manage a degree of surprise. Even in the assessments of the exercise just past, without regard to the problem of the E-boats and the LSTs, General Lee had repeated the warnings:

"Security. General Collins is wisely cautious. A major general has recently been relieved of his command and awaits court-martial because of violation of security. There are no favorites. In North Africa a British Division commander, a man of great promise, was disgraced and relieved of his command because of violations of security. Not a word mentioned outside the conference room. Speak only to a senior officer who is known to you and is Bigoted. As your deputy theater commander I must caution you—in other armies they cut their throats. We can only disgrace you."

If prisoners had been taken by the E-boats, and if they were Bigots, then what was to happen? Frankly, no one knew. The specter of calling off the invasion was raised in General Montgomery's camp. He had already secured its postponement from May until June 5. If it was to be postponed again, then most likely it would have to be held over until the spring of 1945 when the tide and weather conditions would again make it possible. Everyone concerned knew that if the invasion were called off one more time, it was doubtful if it could be staged at all in 1944, and if it were not, then there would be hell to pay with the Russians. They had been suspicious for two years as to the Western Allied intentions and only recently had begun to show any real enthusiasm.

The first task was to find out precisely what had happened. But when the intelligence men began checking the records and interviewing the survivors, they found that as with most disasters, facts were not that easy to come by. The various accounts by the surviving ships' captains (the skippers of *LST 507* and *LST 531* were both lost) did not all tally as to times and events. Not even the number of dead and missing was known precisely, for navy and army records went down with the two vessels. For example, in *LST 507,* the senior army officer present was Captain Seibert. He had brought a roster aboard, but many names had been crossed out. The number of names on the roster was 292, but Captain Seibert had told Lieutenant Murdock, the senior surviving officer of *LST 507,* that the real number of army personnel who actually arrived on the ship was 282. Captain Seibert was among those missing.

Even more worrisome was the story of *LST 531,* for most of the people aboard that vessel had been lost. When the investigators had come up with their best figures here is what they had:

Known Casualties

Sunk	Navy	Army
LST 507		
Aboard	165	282
Rescued	94	151
Killed or Missing	71	131
LST 531		
Aboard	142	354
Rescued	28	44
Killed or Missing	114	310

In addition, aboard *LST 511,* slightly damaged, fourteen men had been wounded. Aboard *LST 289,* which was badly damaged, eight men were missing, along with the five dead and twenty-one sailors and soldiers wounded. Where were the eight? For that matter where were the nearly six hundred dead and missing?

The base of the inquiry was broadened. Were there any Bigots among the missing? The nature of the vessels involved—LSTs—indicated that it was unlikely that high-ranking officers would be aboard. Captain Seibert was the senior army officer aboard *LST 507*, and the number of Bigoted captains was extremely limited. But the intelligence people had the grim realization that no one knew precisely who was aboard the two vessels involved. General Montgomery was a precise commander, known for his advocacy of the "set battle" fought in an orderly fashion with all possible factors known. He first asked the British Admiralty for its assessment, and when the Admiralty announced that there was no way the E-boats could have taken prisoners, because the escorts would have driven them off, Montgomery remained cheerfully skeptical and ordered his own staff to make a new investigation. Involved in this was an American staff officer, Major Ralph Ingersoll, who had been assigned as a liaison officer to General Montgomery's headquarters. On the morning of April 29, Major Ingersoll was ordered to go down to the area and find out what he could about the incident. He went down to Dartmouth and found *LST 289*, moored at her berth, where she would await repairs. But she would never make the coming invasion. There Ingersoll discovered a pair of young army lieutenants who had been aboard *LST 289* when the attack occurred. Ingersoll told the story that was floating around Montgomery's headquarters: how the escorts had driven off the E-boats.

Escorts? What escorts? The lieutenants swore they had not seen hide nor hair of an escort during the whole voyage, that the E-boats were slipping in and out ánd around their formation of waddling LSTs like barn swallows among a flight of crows, and that there was no reason in the world the Germans could not have had all the prisoners they wanted from the hundreds of men struggling in the water from the two sunken vessels. The E-boat that had attacked *LST 289*, they said, had torpedoed them, and then hove to in the darkness outside their little perimeter of light, and turned on its searchlight, which then played on the heads of the men in the water.

This tale has many apocryphal aspects; in the first place, the three LSTs were hit at different times in different places, and, further, no one else is known to have seen the searchlights. But the tale sounded convincing to Ingersoll, who returned to Montgomery's headquarters to report that there had been plenty of time for the Germans to have taken survivors as prisoners if they had been so inclined.

Meanwhile, the intelligence and security people at SHAEF were getting the same sort of information, and they were growing nervous. They ordered a whole new investigation with the object of finding every man who could have had any valuable information. The first step was to send down divers into the wrecks to find the bodies. They found some.

The whole task proved to be Herculean. First, all the bodies had to be identified and the missing found by extrapolation. Since it was not known exactly how many men were missing, this was difficult, if not impossible. Second, as in the tale in which General Huebner figured, the bodies had drifted away from the wrecks, and many had simply disappeared.

But at least an effort could be made to satisfy the investigators—and the SHAEF staff—that the odds against the secret's exposure were high. And that is how the investigation was conducted. Some missing bodies—not all by far—were found. Some dog tags were recovered. Finally, the British Admiralty announced that no prisoners could have been taken, and this time, although there were doubters, the official British naval version was accepted. General Montgomery's investigation indicated that all Bigots were accounted for. As far as SHAEF was concerned, then, security had been maintained.

One reason for this conclusion was that there was no immediate reaction on the other side. The experts at Bletchley Park had been watching the German military traffic. If something had really happened—if prisoners had been taken and their interrogation had revealed the secrets of D-Day—then the Allies could expect an immediate reshuffle of forces, which were at the moment very heavily stacked in the Pas de Calais area. No such messages appeared. No special note was taken by the Germans of the E-boat attack of the night of April 27-28. The German broadcast of the attack simply referred to the sinking of three ships in convoy totaling 19,000 tons. In fact, the action was dwarfed by one the next day: the British 10th Minelaying Flotilla was operating off the Ile de Bas, covered by two motor torpedo boats and the Canadian destroyers *Haida* and *Athabaskan.* The minelaying was just about finished when an enemy destroyer force was plotted off the entrance to the Morlaix River, and the two Canadian destroyers went out to intercept it. They found two Elbing-class German destroyers and opened fire. In the battle that followed one enemy destroyer was driven aground, on fire, but the *Athabaskan* was hit aft and went dead in the water. Apparently she was torpedoed then, because she blew up. So Admiral Ramsay and the others had more on their minds than the problem of the Bigots.

And so for that fact did General Eisenhower and the top officers of SHAEF. On April 30 came really alarming news: the construction of the artificial Mulberry harbors was way behind schedule, and someone raised another nightmare: what if the artificial harbors could not be brought into place in time. Many more tugs than expected would be needed to hurry them into position before Operation Neptune, the crossing of the channel, began. But there was a serious shortage of tugs in Britain, and no one knew how they were going to manage.

There was also that continued serious shortage of LSTs. The reserve of

LSTs of the Allies now was zero. When this problem was brought to Eisenhower's attention by General Bedell Smith, the supreme commander ordered a hot cable sent to the Combined Chiefs of Staff, advising them of the loss and the situation that had developed as a result of the Slapton Sands exercise.

"We are stretched to the limit in the LST category," Eisenhower wrote General Marshall, and he admitted to being worried by the implications of the E-boat attack which had brought about this state of affairs. "The possibility of both raiders and bombers concentrating on some of our important ports makes one scratch his head."

If there was worry at General Montgomery's headquarters about the possible implications of Operation Tiger, Eisenhower had even more pressing matters on his mind. The whole question of security was growing harder, not easier, as thousands upon thousands of men milled about, waiting for that special moment. Journalists, whose task it is to inquire, were giving the military authorities a very bad time. Eisenhower's friend, the Associated Press's Wes Gallagher, came to SHAEF with a mixed-up version of the General Miller case which was true enough in its import—that a high official had been sent home for violating security. But even the mixed-up version could be harmful. Eisenhower found himself constantly hampered by the prying of the press, and by various breaches of censorship discipline.

Just after Operation Tiger the supreme commander blew up when he found himself quoted in the newspapers after making speeches for the troops only. He had issued orders that nothing he said was to be quoted directly or indirectly. After this he refused to allow any newspapermen in the vicinity of the military stations he was inspecting. Nothing was to be permitted that would give the enemy the idea that the invasion was scheduled for a very near date in the future.

As for that enemy, beginning in March 1944, he had been anticipating invasion. That was the month that German intelligence noted the transfer of six British and American divisions from the Mediterranean to England. At that point, Field Marshal Rommel had become convinced that invasion was imminent, and he and Lieutenant General Hans Speidel, his chief of staff, so told Hitler at the first of April. They assured the chief of the German state that it was only a matter of weeks before the blow fell. There were seventy-five divisions in Great Britain, of which they assessed sixty-five as capable of invasion, they said.

Just after the Slapton Sands exercise, the Allies stepped up the bombing of Germany, an act that convinced Rommel that since invasion was nearly upon them, the Allied concentrations of ships and troops should be reconnoitered, attacked, and harassed constantly. He approached Hitler, but nothing happened.

At that point Rommel expected invasion anywhere, against the mouths of the Somme, Bresle, Arques, and Seine, the harbors of Abbeville and Le Havre, the coast of Calvados, or the Cotentin Peninsula, and Cherbourg. Like all other highly placed Germans, he thought the matter of a port was all-important. He could not see how the Allies could attack without taking a port almost immediately.

That is why the Mulberry harbors were so vital to the Allied scheme of attack, and why suddenly SHAEF was shaken by the realization that the Mulberry construction was way behind schedule.

The first pierheads were supposed to be ready at the end of March, but they were not. Rather, they were scarcely more than halfway along. At the end of April they were still not complete, and a force of 300 welders was dragooned from industries throughout Britain and rushed to the scene. On May 10 they finally finished the first five pierheads. Still, by May 15, not all the pierheads were complete. And not by June 1, either. There was no way the invasion could have been carried out at the end of May as had been envisaged early in the year. The new date was June 5.

In order to complete the Mulberry harbors, an enormous emergency work force had to be enlisted on short notice. Twenty-two thousand new workers were brought in, many from neutral Ireland, where pro-German sympathy was not uncommon, thus adding immeasurably to the security risk.

At the beginning of May, Field Marshal Rommel demanded reinforcement of the western area. The prime reason for the demand was the big increase in bombing. He asked for six Panzer divisions to be put at the disposal of his Army Group B. The Inspector General of Panzer forces, Colonel General Heinz Guderian, and General Geyr von Schweppenburg visited Rommel's headquarters, and he told them what he wanted. They raised no objections, but the divisions did not come. They could not come without the specific approval of Hitler, and Hitler was waiting.

Meanwhile, the Allies were making their final preparations for the assault and assessing the disaster on Slapton Sands.

The wrinkles of the whole force were to be worked out in the six Fabius exercises, which followed immediately on the heels of Operation Tiger. Fabius included all five units, the three British groups that would land on the eastern beaches, and American Force U and Force O, which would land on Utah and Omaha.

Fabius I was the exercise of Force O. Fabius II involved the British troops and ships of Force G, bound for Gold Beach. Fabius III involved the Canadians who would assault Juno Beach. Fabius IV was the rehearsal of Force S, British troops bound for Sword Beach. Fabius V was an exercise for the troops who would come to the British beaches after the first assault. Fabius V involved the men of Force B who would reinforce the American beaches. There was, however, no time for another exercise for Force U. The men would have to stand with what they had learned on Slapton Sands and in the days following.

In the disaster off Slapton Sands, most of the casualties had come from *LST 531*. Altogether, the 1st Engineer Special Brigade had suffered most, with 413 lost and 16 wounded. The 3206th Quartermaster Service Company was virtually destroyed. Of 251 officers and men, 201 were killed or wounded. The 557th Quartermaster Railhead Company also lost 69 men.

In fact, even in 1984 no one knew precisely how many men were lost since many of the army's records disappeared during and after the war. The most complete figures were those prepared by the 1st Brigade:

	Killed	Wounded	Missing
Organization			
Hq 1st Eng Sp Brig	2		
531 Eng Shore Reg.	9		10
3206 Qm Sv Co	39	9	156
3207 Qm Sv Co	1		1
607 Graves Reg Co.	6	1	10
462 Amph Tr Co	5		37
478 Amph Tr Co	15	1	13
306 Qm Bn		1	
556 Qm Rhd Co	2	1	1
557 Qm Rhd Co	48	1	25
625 Ord Co	2	1	10
33 Qm Decon Co	10	2	9
1605 Engr Map Dep Dt	3		
	142	16	271

From May 1 the training intensified as much as possible. The Allied high command was determined to iron out its wrinkles. The 1st Engineer Special Brigade was reequipped, and the 3206th Quartermaster Service Company was replaced by the 363rd Quartermaster Service Company. The 557th Quartermaster Railhead Company was replaced by the 562nd Quartermaster Railhead Company.

When the figures were in, they showed that among the dead or missing of the 1st Engineer Special Brigade were fourteen officers. Of these only two, from the headquarters of the 1st Engineer Special Brigade, could have had any special knowledge of the secrets of D-Day, and the bodies of these men had been found. That was as much proof that no dangerous prisoners of war could have been taken by the Germans as the Allies were to get. The security men declared themselves satisfied, and the planning for the June 5 invasion of France went on.

15

Month of Trials

THE RENEWED confidence of the Allied command that the secrets of D-Day had not been compromised in the battle of the LSTs off Slapton Sands was suddenly shaken just a week after the event; the Ultra listeners at Bletchley Park picked up Hitler's new orders for the defense of Normandy.

The orders called for strengthening of the Normandy defenses, and aerial photographs taken that week showed that the orders were being followed. A flurry of enterprise appeared on the beaches of the Calvados coast as Germans and Frenchmen added to the sea obstacles and beach defenses. Agents in France reported on the sudden movement of troops. The 21st Panzer Division moved from Brittany to a point just south of Caen, the objective of Montgomery's 21st Army Group. The Panzer Lehr Division was brought from Hungary to Argentan. The 91st Air Landing Division moved up to the Cotentin Peninsula at La Haye-du-Puits.

This seemed enormously significant because this division's specialty was antiparatroop warfare and it had been spotted right in the middle of the drop zone of the 101st Airborne and 82nd Airborne divisions for D-Day. It now covered the triangle between Bricquebec, St.-Sauveur-le Vicomte, and Ste.-Mère-Eglise. The German 6th Parachute Regiment was also moved up southwest of Carentan.

Further, the 101st Regiment, equipped with flamethrowers, was moved to the coast. The 17th Machine Gun Battalion was moved to the Cap de la Hague, and the 795th Georgian Battalion and the 100th Armored Car Battalion were near Carentan. All these units were warned to watch for enemy airborne landings from this point forward. Suddenly, on the beaches along the Calvados coast and in the fields nearby, began to appear great sowings of "Rommel's asparagus," large poles, capable of smashing up a glider, and topped with antipersonnel mines. It was too late to complete the Todt Organization's most elaborate shore defenses (several reinforced concrete blockhouses stood unfinished on the shore), but barbed wire could be laid quickly, and new trench systems could be dug. They were.

The concern went all the way up the SHAEF command. The whole question of security was opened again. But there was no direct evidence that the security of Operation Overlord had been breached, and some that it had not, despite the fears of the Ultra people. For example, Field Marshal von Rundstedt's headquarters gave no signs of concern, and there was no panic movement of troops out of the Pas de Calais area toward the west. General Sepp Dietrich's 1 SS Panzer Corps, the most powerful unit available to the Germans along the Atlantic Wall, remained as it was, part of it at Toulouse, and part near Antwerp. Some of the British argued for abandonment of the whole cross-channel attack, but they were overruled. However, the two American airborne divisions did revise their drop zones to avoid the newly arrived enemy troops.

Otherwise the plan remained. June 5 was still D-Day. It was a brave decision taken without any real knowledge of what was happening across the channel. The fact was that it was also a shrewd decision. All the flap on the other side had been caused by Hitler's exercise of his famous intuition. He awakened one morning and simply decided that he ought to strengthen the Normandy area, and so he issued orders. There had been no breach.

Hardly had the dust from this scare settled, when another crisis appeared. Operation Fortitude, the main Allied deception operation, was proceeding splendidly with every indication that field marshals von Rundstedt and Rommel, and even Hitler, were guessing that the Pas de Calais would be the scene of the real Allied thrust no matter what happened initially.

One near mistake was the Allied air destruction of the Seine River bridges that month. Field Marshal von Rundstedt, who had been opting for the Pas de Calais attack, suddenly began to have a feeling that Normandy had to be watched, but that feeling died down as the air attacks on the Pas de Calais region increased.

Admiral Theodor Krancke, the director of naval defenses along the channel coast, had virtually written off the Normandy area as the scene of attack because of the shallows, currents, and tides. He still looked north to Norway with anxiety.

Then, from Lisbon, came startling information.

About a year earlier, the Double Cross Committee had enlisted the services of a member of the Abwehr who was guaranteed to MI 6 to be an anti-Nazi. He was given the code name Artist, and he joined the ring of Dusko Popov, a Yugoslavian businessman who had worked diligently and successfully for the British for four years. Popov's ring had been extremely influential in persuading the Germans of the actual existence of General George S. Patton's First Army Group, that mythical military body that camouflage and radio deception had created in the southeastern English countryside.

Then Erich Vermehren, the Abwehr's principal agent in Ankara, defected to the Allies. The shock waves reached Lisbon, where Vermehren's mother lived. The agent Artist was known to be a frequent caller at her house, and he was kidnapped by Abwehr agents, smuggled to Germany in a trunk, and interrogated by the Gestapo, which meant torture. From that point until the invasion the Double Cross Committee expected at any moment to learn that the whole deception plan had been blown.

May was a month of trials. Nearly every day it seemed, someone unearthed a bit of information that boded ill for the coming invasion of France. One day, browsing in the second-hand book shops off London's St. Martin's Lane, an officer of the 101st Airborne Division came across a book titled *Paratroopers,* written by a Czechoslovak army captain. It was a resume of early German airborne operations and included a chapter on the possible uses of airborne forces by the Allies. The "hypothetical" plan called for the dropping of paratroops on the Cotentin Peninsula near Cherbourg. The drop zones were almost precisely those planned by the 101st Airborne and the 82nd Airborne divisions. More worry.

By mid-May worries simply had to be disregarded. The time had come to put the operation on or off, the troops were now all concentrated in the marshaling areas. By that time division commanders were allowed to reveal the division plans—but not the date of the operation—to regimental and battalion commanders. Those officers, in turn, were allowed to brief a few of their key subordinates. Once the troops were locked in the "sausages," the plans were opened up. Sand tables and three-dimensional maps showed the whole Cherbourg Peninsula. Major General Maxwell D. Taylor, commander of the 101st Airborne Division, made all his troops study the maps, and not just the area where they were supposed to drop. In Sicily, he remembered, the paratroops had been dropped far from their destination. The men should have some feeling for the whole peninsula so they would be able to make their ways to the proper areas.

But, of course, as the men were briefed on the terrain, the secret of D-Day passed into thousands of new hands. The only way to turn back now would be to scrap the invasion plan entirely, and that would mean a delay of at least a year in opening the second front, a thought completely inimical to President Roosevelt and the American Joint Chiefs of Staff. Operation Overlord would go on.

One morning in May at the British War Office a gust of wind picked up all twelve copies of a secret communiqué that gave away the when and where of the invasion and swirled them out the window and down into the street below. Staff officers scurried down the stairs and began searching the pavement. They found eleven copies. The twelfth had disappeared. The alarm went out, but later in the day that twelfth copy was handed over to a sentry on the opposite side of the Whitehall complex. A search was made for the civilian who had handed over the plan, a middle-aged man with thick glasses, but he was never found.

A railway conductor picked up a briefcase in a train, and inside were plans for the invasion of Normandy. He gave them to the station master at Exeter, and the station master put the plans in his safe and called the Home Guard, who sent sentries. The safe was well guarded until a staff officer from SHAEF came up the next day to pick up the briefcase. The conductor of the train said nothing about the matter until 1957. Thus were the secrets of SHAEF preserved.

Still, General Eisenhower continued to be upset by indications that SHAEF security was less than it ought to be during these last troublesome, fretful days. On May 21 the supreme commander received a complaint against Captain Wright of the staff of Admiral Stark, commander of U.S. Naval Forces in Europe.

Again it came from Air Chief Marshal Leigh-Mallory. Again it was strong and specious.

> That Captain Wright attended a party at the house of a Mr. Dupree, at which were present a number of people, including civilians, among whom were several servants. It is alleged that Captain Wright, apparently intoxicated, revealed details of impending operations to include areas, lift, strength, and dates.

Poor Captain Wright. It was May 1944. Eisenhower was under the most intense sort of pressure. Captain Wright never had a chance.

"I have been disturbed, not to say alarmed, by a report involving Captain Wright. . . ." wrote Eisenhower to Admiral Stark. "If this report is even partially true, and in view of the number of witnesses given by the man making the report it would appear that there is little reason to doubt that it is, then I must say that the greatest harm could result from this indiscretion. . . ." wrote Eisenhower to Admiral Stark.

And, of course, Admiral Stark had no alternative.

"Am sending Wright home. I see no alternative. He will be a distinct loss and I have no replacement at present, but that can't be helped," Stark wrote the supreme commander.

"No need to go into the details of it, though the evidence to my mind is clear that Wright was not intoxicated and that much of the conversation that took place was common newspaper knowledge. However that is one thing. Wright saying it is another. At any rate I have told Wright that his usefulness here is at an end. . . ."

Not quite so stern an end as that of General Miller, but a sort of disgrace nonetheless, and one that again left many people wondering how many personal vendettas were being satisfied under the guise of "security."

Eisenhower seemed not to notice the undercurrents. He could not. His whole attention was devoted to the task that would be at hand in only a matter of days and to thinking past the invasion itself.

He wrote General Marshall:

"In forecasting future possibilities it is . . . necessary to seek ways and means to bring to bear those factors in which we enjoy a great superiority over the enemy. These are control of the sea, command of the air, including resources in airborne troops, and armor. I am trying to visualize an operation in which we would bring in behind the initial beachhead a great strength in armor and seek an opportunity to launch a big armored attack in conjunction with a deep and very heavy penetration by airborne troops. . . . Such an operation might be accompanied also by an additional amphibious affair. I have already instructed the staff to look into this possibility because I believe that in some such movement, promising surprise from three directions, and in great strength, we might accomplish a lot. . . ."

Security . . . planning . . . the future. All these matters became paramount at SHAEF headquarters in the last two weeks of May. There was the continued concern lest the British fail to deliver the concrete caissons known as Phoenixes and the other parts of the great Mulberry harbors on time, but in their quixotic way, the British smiled and said they were muddling along and would make it, and there was not much more that could be done. Already it was too late for the American naval forces to have any chance of exercises or practices with the Mulberries. They would be towed across the channel for D-Day, and the men assigned to them would have to make them work somehow.

As for the troops, they were in their "sausages." And once in, there was only one way out. One young lieutenant of the 1st Division had fallen in love with an English girl, all the permissions for their marriage had been secured, and the wedding was set. Then the unit had orders to move to the marshaling area, and that was that. The lieutenant and his friends importuned higher authority. They secured justice of a sort: the lieutenant was taken out of the "sausage" by military police, accompanied to the town where his fiancée waited, and they were married in the church. One kiss, and the lieutenant went back to his "sausage."

The days went on. May drifted away and June began. The German supply system staggered under the heavy blows of the Allied air forces, and Field Marshal Rommel knew that the enemy was coming very soon. Von Rundstedt was complaining to Berlin that locomotives were in such short supply that he wanted to employ prisoners of war on repair work. His headquarters had now decided that the attacks on the Seine River bridges indicated the landings would come near Dieppe. And soon. An air raid on May 31 cut the Paris–Rouen telephone cable so badly that communications broke down for three days.

June 1 found the Germans as undecided as ever where the attack would come, and precisely when it would come. They had expected it during the past month, and nothing had happened. Admiral Krancke now indicated his belief that the next possible date would be in August. Aerial bombardments and Allied propaganda continued to point toward landings in the Pas de Calais. Rommel, for one, found it hard to believe that the enemy would "ram his head against the hardest spot in the defense just for the sake of a short sea voyage." He had now concluded that the landings would come several in succession or simultaneously in a number of places. He half expected a feint and then a major landing. At his headquarters officers spoke of the coast between the Somme River and the Bay of St. Malo. Others mentioned the banks of the Gironde and the Mediterranean coast of France. Some said the banks of the Rhone would first see the Allies.

The where was of utmost importance to the Germans because of Hitler's latest directives to the western defense command: the decisive action must be fought along the Atlantic Wall. The defense must be made on the coast, and the main line of resistance there must be held at all costs.

Rommel knew that the Allies would almost immediately turn to drive on Paris. Given his own head he would have kept his defenses loose, so he could make the most use of them when he knew what the situation was going to be. But even the knowledge of current events was denied him, because Rommel's headquarters depended for its intelligence material on von Rundstedt's headquarters, which depended for its information on Berlin. Thus by denying his subordinates the tool of intelligence, Hitler held the materials of command in his own hands. Just recently, Admiral Canaris had been deposed and his Abwehr disgraced because of its inability to pinpoint the Allied actions. Heinrich Himmler had now taken over the intelligence function, and had politicized it even further than before and made intelligence of less use to the military forces.

Very near the end, as the invasion units waited for the appearance of the Mulberry harbor, it was discovered that the big caissons were in effect stuck in the mud, and it seemed doubtful if they could be moved at all—ever. Fortunately, at this moment appeared Commodore Edward Ellsberg, an American salvage expert. He discovered that the Royal Engineers did not know their job. The matter was so serious that it was referred to the Prime Minister for solution, and he turned the task over to the Royal Navy, which would have American help in solving the insoluble problem.

This all happened on May 21. By May 27 the facilities for pumping out the stuck Phoenixes were in hand. The salvagers would have eight days in which to float the caissons and get them ready to go to France.

On May 28, everybody concerned with the Allied invasion was suddenly sealed inside his camp. No more mail went out. No more came in. The soldiers of the invasion force were effectively prisoners until they moved out across the channel.

It was not until June 2, just three days before the announced D-Day, that the Royal Navy could say it would have the first Mulberry units moving according to schedule.

On June 2 General Eisenhower arose from a restless sleep in his trailer in the hazel grove and went to Southwick House for a weather briefing. The meteorologists were not at all certain what sort of weather they would be having for D-Day. The trouble was that the really good weather of May was now being replaced by some distinctly stormy signs.

From that moment on weather was the determining factor of the invasion. The 5,300 ships and vessels were ready. The troops were either preparing to board vessels, or were already aboard, waiting to be taken to The Far Shore. June 5 was to be D-Day, but only weather permitting.

That day, June 2, the first warships sailed from Scapa Flow, Belfast, and the Clyde River, heading toward the English Channel, needing that much head start to make it in time. Two midget submarines set out from Portsmouth Harbor, bound for The Far Shore where they would mark the assault area for the British craft.

On Saturday, June 3, the weather began acting up. A westerly wind was blowing along the channel. Cloud was expected, and the outlook for Monday, D-Day, was distinctly unfavorable. The decision would have to be made by Sunday morning. Everywhere in the southwest, ships were loading, and men were moving. The whole impetus of England was pushing for the move across the channel.

On Saturday evening at 9:30, the RAF meteorologist announced gloomily that three new depressions seemed to be heading for the channel. His four-day forecast showed rain, high winds, and fog. It was hardly what was wanted.

Someone suggested postponement of the operation. Eisenhower said no, let Force U and Force O sail from their ports as planned. They could always be called back.

And so the ships sailed and headed out into the wind and wave. The SHAEF crew met again at 4:30 on Sunday morning, and the meteorologist was so gloomy that Eisenhower postponed the invasion for twenty-four hours, and the ships that had started forth were told to turn back. Some of them had to be collected. One group very nearly got to the point of making a turn that would head them directly for Normandy, and had any Germans been watching, they might have guessed the secret then.

But no Germans were watching. The dirty weather kept the German observation planes down and the E-boats and destroyers in their harbors. Force U very nearly did not make it back into Weymouth Bay in time to reform to go out again.

Sunday, June 4, brought clear skies, even sunshine, but from afar came the weather report that counted. On June 6, the new D-Day, the cloud and the rain and the wind would be back again.

At nine o'clock on Sunday night the meteorologist reported a gloomy future for D-Day, but with just a touch of hope. On Tuesday, June 6, during the daylight hours, the weather should show a break over the channel. It would close in again by nightfall, but there was a chance to get ashore.

It was either go or scrap the invasion. The ships at sea would not have enough fuel to last until June 7. There was no time to put them into port for supply. Some men had already been aboard vessels for a week or more. By June 8 the tides would be all wrong, and they would continue to be wrong for weeks. It was June 6, or nothing.

So at 4:30 on the morning of June 5, Eisenhower made the fateful decision, and the invasion was on. In a matter of hours, the men of Force U would show what they had learned in the last few months about amphibious operations, and particularly what had been gained or lost in the effort at Slapton Sands.

16

The Proof
of the Pudding

AS THE ships sailed for France, and the airmen and the airborne troops gathered for their final briefings on June 5, 1944, the men were given one-page leaflets marked at the top with the flaming sword device of the Allied Expeditionary Force.

Soldiers, Sailors, and Airmen of the Allied Expeditionary Force!

You are about to embark upon the Great Crusade, toward which we have striven these many months. The eyes of the world are upon you. The hopes and prayers of liberty-loving people everywhere march with you. In company with our brave Allies and brothers-in-arms on other Fronts, you will bring about the destruction of the German war machine, the elimination of Nazi tyranny over the oppressed peoples of Europe, and security for ourselves in a free world.

Your task will not be an easy one. Your enemy is well trained, well equipped and battle-hardened. He will fight savagely.

But this is the year 1944! Much has happened since the Nazi triumphs of 1940-41. The United Nations have inflicted upon the Germans great defeats in open battle, man-to-man. Our air offensive has seriously reduced their strength in the air and their capacity to wage war on the ground. Our Home Fronts have given us an overwhelming superiority in weapons and munitions of war, and placed at our disposal great reserves of trained fighting men. The tide has turned! The free men of the world are marching together to Victory!

I have full confidence in your courage, devotion to duty, and skill in battle. We will accept nothing less than full Victory!

Good luck! And let us all beseech the blessing of Almighty God upon this great and noble undertaking.

Dwight D. Eisenhower.

And in England that day, many watched from high points on the shore as the vessels that had filled the seventeen-mile sweep of Weymouth Bay by the hundreds moved out. Many a man and woman watched all day as ship followed ship, until by evening when dusk fell all of them were gone. That night in pubs all around England the bottled beer and daily whiskey ration stood on the shelves for the first time in a year. England was strangely silent, and the thoughts of many a man and woman turned that night to the enterprise on which their sons, brothers, and cousins from across the sea were bound. "A lot of men are going to die tonight," said one Englishman, and he prayed for them before he went to bed.

As that Englishman slept, the C-47 transport planes bearing the paratroops of the 101st Airborne and 82nd Airborne divisions droned on toward France. They were committed to battle, six parachute regiments and support troops, 13,000 men in 822 transports. The gliders would come in at dawn.

In Exercise Tiger at Slapton Sands, the 101st Airborne Division had been assigned the mission of taking the high ground west of Slapton Sands beginning at H-5 hour on D-Day in support of the 4th Division landings that would come five hours later. They were to seize the road center at Mounts and cross the River Avon at New Bridge, then move south of Aveton Gifford to protect the southern flank of VII Corps.

The troops had begun arriving in the general area of Kingsbridge, East Allington, Loddiswell, and Churchstow at 2:30 A.M. Fourteen minutes later the jumps were completed in the drop zone, and assembly of all units in a neat order had begun within an hour and a half. The troops moved toward their objectives. Only the 3rd Battalion of the 506th Parachute Infantry Regiment met opposition.

The 502nd Parachute Infantry Regiment with the 377th Parachute Field Artillery Battalion was assigned to move east and capture the strong point of Merrifield and then attack southeast to secure the beach exits at Slapton Sands.

The 506th Parachute Infantry, except for the 3rd Battalion, was to move southeast and secure the high ground around Stokenham. The 321st Glider Field Artillery Battalion was to be its support force.

The 3rd Battalion of the 506th, with part of Company C of the 326th Airborne Engineer Battalion, was to move southwest to take the coastline between Salcombe and Thurlestone.

The 501st Parachute Infantry, without its 3rd Battalion, was to move northwest and take the crossroads at Mounts and the bridges at New Bridge and Aveton Gifford. The rest of Company C of the 326th Engineers would be with that unit, plus the 907th Field Artillery Battalion.

The 3rd Battalion of the 501st Parachute Infantry was in reserve, but it had the mission of securing the glider landing zones north of Kingsbridge.

5 A.M.: The parachutists and the division command posts and the division artillery were all in operation.

6:45: The gliders began landing. Fifteen minutes later they were all down.

7:35: All glider elements were in position.

8:00: The 501st Parachute Infantry seized its objectives without opposition. The 502nd and the 506th were held up by opposition.

10:40: The division artillery delivered its concentration of fire on the enemy strong point at Merrifield.

The 506th Parachute Infantry began its attack to secure the beach exits in its area. They were secured at 11:15.

11:00: The 502nd attacked. The attack was successful, and the strong point was in U.S. hands by 11:39. The 502nd then moved to secure the beach exits.

1:50 P.M.: First contact was made with elements of the 4th Division.

2:00: The 502nd and the 506th were relieved by elements of the 4th Division. They assembled and prepared to move west. The first phase of the attack had succeeded in about twelve hours.

That had been the exercise, carried out on a replica of the Norman coast on April 27, 1944.

But on June 6, 1944, came the reality.

At 1:30 in the morning, Germans at St. Floxel, east of Montebourg, heard large numbers of aircraft approaching. Lieutenant Colonel Hoffman, commander of the 3rd Battalion of the 919th Regiment of the 709th Division listened as the noise grew louder. At 2 A.M. six airplanes flying at 500 feet approached his headquarters and dropped parachutists directly on it. Hoffman and his troops rushed out to open fire. The first action between troops of the 101st Airborne Division and the Germans began.

As at Slapton Sands, the primary mission of the 101st Airborne was to seize the western edge of the land area behind the beaches, this time between St. Martin-de-Varreville and Pouppeville. The secondary mission was to protect

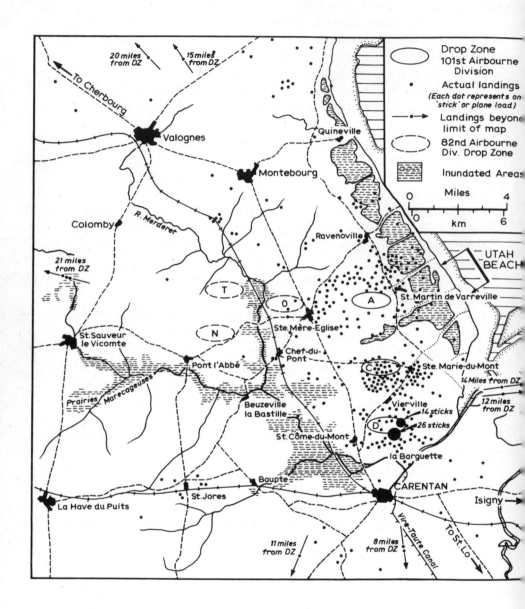

20 miles from DZ

15 miles from DZ

To Cherbourg

Quineville

Valognes

Montebourg

Colomby

R. Merderet

Ravenoville

21 miles from DZ

UTAH BEACH

St.Martin de Varreville

St.Sauveur le Vicomte

T

O

A

N

Ste.Mère-Eglise

Chef-du-Pont

Pont l'Abbé

C

Ste.Marie-du-Mont

14 Miles from DZ

12 miles from DZ

Prairies Marecageuses

Beuzeville la Bastille

Vierville — 14 sticks

D — 26 sticks

St.Côme-du-Mont

la Barguette

Baupte

CARENTAN

La Haye du Puits

St.Jores

Isigny

To St.Lo

Vire-Taute Canal

11 miles from DZ

8 miles from DZ

Drop Zone
101st Airbourne
Division

• Actual landings
(Each dot represents one 'stick' or plane load)

Landings beyond
limit of map

82nd Airbourne
Div. Drop Zone

Inundated Areas

Miles   0 ——— 4

km   0 ——— 6

the southern flank of VII Corps and to move south through Carentan. Two bridges were to be destroyed on the main Carentan highway and the railroad bridge west of it. The La Barquette lock was to be seized and a bridgehead established over the Douve River northeast of Carentan. It was not a precise recreation of the Slapton Sands exercise, because the drop zone had been changed with the knowledge that the Germans had moved troops around, but it was close enough. Instead of Merrifield, the 502nd's mission was to take the enemy coastal battery near St. Martin-de-Varreville, secure the two northern beach exits to the causeway, and establish a defense line linking with the 82nd Airborne Division on the west.

The 506th's beach exits were not called Slapton and Stokenham, as on the exercise maps, but were the two southern exits to the French causeway.

As the planes came over, the 502nd's regimental headquarters and the 2nd Battalion were in the lead. The leading pilots were lost in the clouds and disturbed by antiaircraft fire. Nobody had ever told them it was going to be like this. Consequently, their care in dropping the troops was less than great. Most of the 2nd Battalion was dropped far away from the drop zone. The officers spent most of the day trying to assemble the battalion, and it took no organized part in the fighting.

The 1st Battalion of the 502nd landed in the center of the drop zone near St. Germain-de-Varreville. Lieutenant Colonel Patrick J. Cassidy, the battalion leader, had the problem of collecting men, because the drop had scattered them. He did collect some and moved toward a group of stone buildings at the eastern edge of Mesieres. Here, intelligence reports said, lived the German unit that manned the St. Martin coastal battery that was their main point of attack. These buildings were attacked by a small group of men who moved from one building to another. Staff Sergeant Harrison Summers led the attack, rushing into the first building, kicking open doors, and spraying the rooms with his submachine gun. Moving from room to room and building to building, he and a few others killed about 150 Germans.   *(about 15)?*

Lieutenant Colonel John H. Michaelis, the 502nd Regiment commander, showed up with about 200 men late in the afternoon. Colonel Cassidy had gathered more men and established a defensive line at Foucarville. They established four roadblocks. The Germans, on a hill to the northwest, attacked them all day long.

The 3rd Battalion of the 502nd dropped in the wrong place, too, east of Ste.-Mère-Eglise. Luckily, Lieutenant Colonel Robert G. Cole knew where he was and began moving toward St. Martin-de-Varreville, his objective. Using artificial crickets as a recognition signal, Colonel Cole managed to assemble 75 men (the battalion numbered about 800). Some of them were not even his men, but 82nd Airborne troops who had *really* been dropped in the wrong place.

They reached the coastal gun battery with only a few skirmishes, but then discovered that it was all in vain: the Germans had moved the battery and the position was deserted. Cole then took the men to the causeway exit at Audouville-la-Hubert. They took position there to protect the causeway exit from enemy attack down onto the beaches. They were in position by 7:30 A.M. Two hours later Germans retreating from the 4th Division assault on the beach came up the causeway exit, and the paratroopers shot them down. At 1 P.M. they made contact with the troops of the 4th Division.

Except for the bad drop and the failure of intelligence which had caused them to waste time on the attack on the battery position, the experience of the 502nd Parachute Infantry was just about as it had been on Slapton Sands. The remainder of the regiment had not appeared, but with the German desertion of the battery position they had not been needed anyhow.

Like the 502nd Parachute Infantry, the 506th was badly scattered in the airdrop. However, two hours later Colonel Robert F. Sink, the regimental commander, had more or less brought them together. The regiment's mission was almost a carbon copy of the Slapton Sands exercise. Change the names Slapton and Stokenham to Houdienville and Pouppeville, and that was the assignment: take and hold the southern beach exits from the causeway.

The trouble was that this part of the mission belonged to the 2nd Battalion, and that battalion was dropped completely outside its zone. Lieutenant Colonel Robert L. Strayer gathered men and swept out, but he never made it. He was held up at the first objective, Houdienville, all morning by enemy machine gun fire.

Colonel Sink established his command post at Culoville, and when he learned that the beach exits were not under control, he sent the 1st Battalion to Pouppeville. They, too, were held up.

Major General Maxwell D. Taylor, the division commander, learned that the Pouppeville and Houdienville exits were not manned and sent the 3rd Battalion of the 501st Parachute Infantry to do the job. The 3rd Battalion had been designated as the division reserve and was supposed to secure the glider landing zones. For them nothing worked out according to plan. Lieutenant Colonel Julian Ewell learned that three planes carrying 3rd Battalion troops had been shot down, causing the loss of many men. Still, Colonel Ewell gathered enough men to send about fifty to the Pouppeville beach exit, and they arrived at 8 A.M. The Germans were there. They fought, and at noon the Germans surrendered. The Americans had suffered eighteen casualties, the Germans twenty-five. The Americans had captured thirty-eight prisoners. The rest of the Germans retreated toward the beach, where they ran into the 4th Division's troops and surrendered. So while the 506th Parachute Infantry had not carried out its mission, the 501st had done so. The fact was that the 506th had dropped into the center of a large German concentration and was isolated there all of D-Day, until finally elements of the 4th Division broke through near Holdy late in the afternoon.

So at the end of D-Day, the 101st Airborne Division had secured the western edge of Utah Beach. That was part of the mission. The other part was to occupy the line of the Douve River on both sides of Carentan and to protect the southern flank of VII Corps, and then to drive south through Carentan to put together the VII Corps and V Corps beachheads.

The 3rd Battalion of the 506th Parachute Infantry had succeeded nicely in moving southwest during Operation Tiger to seize the English coastline between Salcombe and Thurlestone. The 907th Field Artillery Battalion had shown up right on schedule and was in support. That was April.

In June, when the performance was repeated in Normandy, the battalion found that the first objective was Vierville and the second, Le Port. The drop was south of Vierville. But at that point the Germans were waiting; they had put up an antiaircraft barrage that hit a number of planes and had illuminated the drop zone by setting fire to a building in the middle of it. Some paratroopers landed to be greeted by concentrated machine gun fire. Others landed in the swamp east of the drop zone. Captain Charles G. Shettle collected some officers and men and reached the bridge at Brevands. They established themselves on the river bank and held. It was a most tenuous position, saved only by the failure of the Germans to counterattack.

According to the plan, the 501st, less its 3rd Battalion, was to seize the lock at La Barquette, blow the bridges on the St. Come-du-Mont—Carentan road, take St. Come-du-Mont and destroy the railroad bridge to the west. In the exercise at Slapton Sands the regiment had easily completed its mission by 8 A.M. In the reality their airdrop was a mess, and the commanding officer and staff of the 1st Battalion were lost in a plane crash. All the company commanders were gone. Fortunately, Colonel Howard R. Johnson, the regimental commander, dropped in the area, and he undertook the mission. But it was no picnic, as it had been in England, and they never did manage to blow the Douve bridges that day. They did take and hold the lock at La Barquette, which was the essential element of their task.

At the end of the day, the 101st Airborne Division had managed to bring

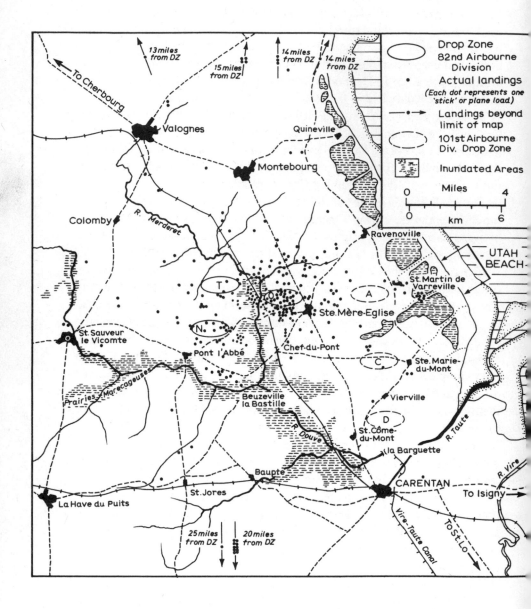

⬭	Drop Zone 82nd Airbourne Division
•	Actual landings *(Each dot represents one 'stick' or plane load)*
•–•–•	Landings beyond limit of map
⬭	101st Airbourne Div. Drop Zone
▦	Inundated Areas

Miles
0 — 4
0 — 6
km

To Cherbourg

13 miles from DZ
15 miles from DZ
14 miles from DZ
14 miles from DZ

Valognes
Quineville
Montebourg
Colomby
R. Merderet
Ravenoville
UTAH BEACH
St. Martin de Varreville
T
O
A
Ste. Mère-Eglise
St. Sauveur le Vicomte
N
Chef-du-Pont
C
Ste. Marie-du-Mont
Pont l'Abbé
Prairies Marecageuses
Beuzeville la Bastille
Vierville
D
St. Côme-du-Mont
R. Douve
la Barguette
R. Taute
Baupte
La Haye du Puits
St. Jores
CARENTAN
R. Vire
To Isigny
Vire-Taute Canal
To St. Lo
25 miles from DZ
20 miles from DZ

into assembly only 2,500 of the 6,000 men who had dropped from the air. Even so, they had managed to clear the way for the move of the 4th Division inland, and that was the whole reason for their inclusion in the operation. To accomplish this the 101st Airborne Division had suffered 1,240 casualties that first day.

The 82nd Airborne Division suffered even more severely due to the incompetence of the airdrop. The troop carrier pilots were green, many of them had never seen antiaircraft fire before and when it began hitting their planes, some panicked. That was one of the problems that could not have been solved at Slapton Sands.

The 82nd Airborne's tasks were to capture Ste.-Mère-Eglise, hold both sides of the Merderet River, clear the area between the sea and the river, and the area from the Douve River north to Ste.-Mère-Eglise.

But with many troopers drowned in the swamps near the coast, many others bogged down there, and many lost, the only mission carried out according to plan was the capture of Ste.-Mère-Eglise, and that was because the 505th Parachute Infantry was dropped precisely where it was supposed to go at the time it was supposed to be there. The others were dropped all over Normandy, and as they grouped up, they encountered the enemy and got involved in fighting. Oddly enough, the very inefficiency of the American airdrop contributed to its overall success in a manner never envisaged at Slapton Sands: the Germans were thoroughly confused by so many reports of so many paratroopers coming down in so many places, and instead of mounting one or two considered counterattacks to isolate the troops on the beaches from the shore, the Germans made many forays at different points, using limited numbers of troops and bogging down in battle with the para-troopers. At the end of the day, the 82nd Airborne was in distinct command of Ste.-Mère-Eglise, but held precariously a number of other small positions. It had no contact with the 101st Airborne as had been expected. It had no contact with the 4th Division. Its casualties were 1,259 men.

17

The Lessons
Learned

H-HOUR WAS set for 6:30 on the morning of June 6, 1944. There would be no postponement; Admiral Moon had learned his lesson at Slapton Sands.

The convoy headed for Utah Beach moved along steadily through the choppy sea, although the six-foot waves stirred by the 20-knot wind made it rough going for the LCIs and smaller craft. Visibility was about eight miles with a cloud ceiling at 10,000 feet. Up above the men in the ships could see the comforting forms of fighter planes that provided an umbrella against air and sea attack.

There was no attack, by E-boats or anyone else, so none of the men got a chance to show how well they had learned the lessons of proper wearing of the life vests. The Germans were blissfully unaware of the Allied coming. In fact, Field Marshal Rommel, seeing what a foul day had dawned on June 5, and being informed that the bad weather would continue, had taken off for his home at Ulm in Germany for a short surprise visit to his family. The naval forces at Le Havre and Cherbourg were somnolent. It was not the sort of day to be out in an E-boat facing seas that poured in over the bow and shook the long slender boats as they smashed down on the decking. The foul weather had prevented the Luftwaffe from scheduling reconnaissance missions. Even the German army in Normandy had chosen this weather "respite" to schedule a briefing for divisional commanders to instruct them in antiparatroop tactics, and they were away from their posts.

As the invasion force neared the land, the weather grew worse, and the air ceiling lower. After Slapton Sands, the airmen had agreed to plaster the

181

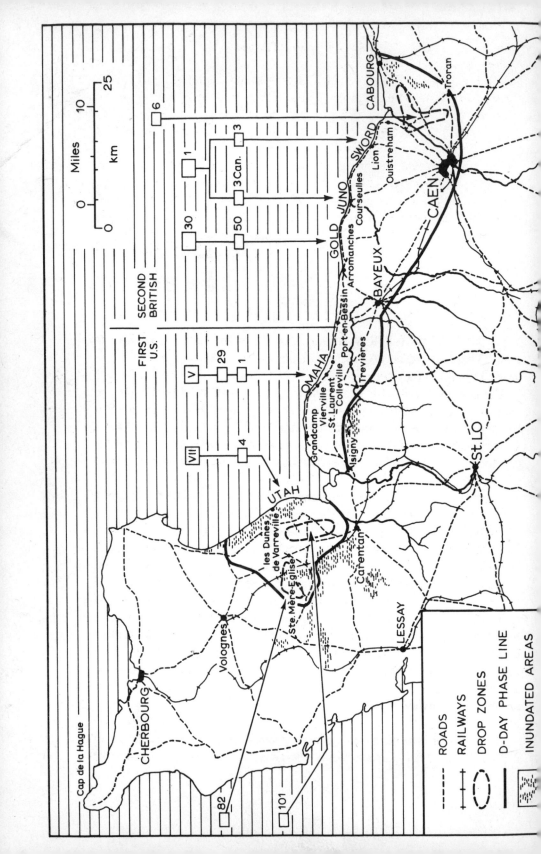

Cap de la Hague

CHERBOURG

Volognes

UTAH

les Dunes de Varreville

Ste-Mère-Eglise

82

101

LESSAY

Carentan

VII

4

FIRST
U.S.

V

29

1

OMAHA

Grandcamp
Vierville
St.-Laurent
Colleville

Port-en-Bessin
Isigny
Trevières

St. LO

Miles
0   10   25
0   km

SECOND
BRITISH

30

50

1

3 Can.

3

6

GOLD

JUNO

SWORD

CABOURG

Troran

Arromanches
Courseulles
Lion
Ouistreham

BAYEUX

CAEN

ROADS

RAILWAYS

DROP ZONES

D-DAY PHASE LINE

INUNDATED AREAS

beaches of Normandy with big bombs from heavy bombers, but this morning when the bombers came over, the beaches were hidden beneath the cloud cover, so they were forced to bomb by instrument. The beaches were untouched, the 13,000 bombs fell as far as three miles inland, and whatever they hit was completely by mistake. The medium bombers came in later, beneath the overcast, but the pilots had no experience at this sort of thing, and a third of the bombs fell in the sea, and most of the others did no damage to the German defenses along the Atlantic Wall. The airmen could have done with a little of that combined training they had resisted until after Operation Tiger, when it was too late.

At 2:30 in the morning Admiral Moon's command ship *Bayfield* dropped anchor in the transport area about fifteen miles off the French beach— another lesson learned at Slapton Sands: anchoring in too close would bring trouble.

At 3 A.M. the Germans suddenly came awake with a report that a number of vessels had been sighted in the Bay of the Seine. From Le Havre the torpedo boats went out, but they were attacked from the air as they tried to attack a group of destroyers, the E-boats ran out of torpedoes and had to return to base for more. At Cherbourg the E-boats were held up by the tide, and when two of them went out to reconnoiter, they met such heavy seas they had to turn back to port.

The German coastal batteries along the Bay of the Seine were also alerted and began firing on the ships of Force O off Omaha Beach and those of Force U. The time was 5:35 A.M. The naval force was far enough out at sea that the coastal fire was ineffective.

At 6 A.M. the Allied naval bombardment began. The troops had gotten out of their transports and into LCVPs and DUKWs and were heading in to shore. The shells flew over their heads. There was no question about the bombardment this time. It was there in comforting strength.

As the boats headed in a handful of German fighter planes appeared over Force U and swooped down to attack. Immediately they were "bounced" by Spitfires from above and shot down or driven off. The air support had arrived on schedule.

Ahead of the landing craft the gunboats and rocket boats sped in to shore. The gunboats carried 4.7-inch guns. They were shooting up into the dunes. No question of lackadaisical performance this time. Seventeen of the gunboats were equipped with rocket launchers. After the rocket failure at Slapton Sands, their skippers had been told to hold their fire until it would be effective, and that was what they did. The 50-pound rockets blew up on the beaches.

Some of the boats were knocked out by shore fire. Some of them sped in, gamely firing. The performance was not perfect, but it was a great deal better than it had been at Slapton Sands.

At 6:30 the boats began landing troops. An amphibious tank sank just offshore, a reminder of the one Commander Butcher had watched go down off Slapton Sands. There had been no way to perfect them, the engineers had found. Thirty-two of the amphibians were launched that morning. The whole operation was delayed because their control vessel struck a mine, and three more went down.

The 8th Infantry regiment was to go in first, occupy the high ground along the road between Ste.-Màrie-du-Mont and Les Forges and then move across the Merderet River to join up with the 82nd Airborne Division. One battalion would move west of St. Martin to protect the north flank until the 22nd Infantry arrived. That regiment would land at H+85 and seize the causeway at les Dunes de Varreville, then seize the high ground at Quineville.
In the center, Colonel Russell P. Reeder's 8th Infantry would advance to seize the high ground between Edmondeville and the Merderet River.
That was the plan. It had all worked very nicely for the 4th Division at Slapton Sands, except for the problem of the engineers and the beaches, and the engineers had been told all about that.

The LCVPs of the 8th Infantry's two assault battalions hit the beach. The men were looking for the windmill and the small patch of dunes higher than the others—this identified les Dunes de Varreville. The LCVPs ground to a stop and the men began moving off. Some of the LCVPs were putting the men off in four feet of water. They were about a hundred yards from the edge of the sand. They had been told to expect heavy fire from the defenders, but there was almost no noise. A few men fell, the victims of artillery fire, but not many. Soon the men reached the edge of the sand, and a seawall four feet high. No high dunes. No windmill. None of the landmarks they were supposed to see were on the maps; they had landed in the wrong place.
After Operation Tiger, when some men had been landed in the wrong place at the wrong time, an officer had asked Admiral Moon if at the time of the actual invasion the navy would guarantee to put them ashore in the right place. That was the navy's job, said the admiral, but one could never guarantee against slipups.
This time, at Utah Beach, the assault element had come in more than a mile south of the designated area. The reason or reasons involved a combination of

circumstances. The landing craft had been led in on their long run by two 173-foot patrol boats and one smaller boat fitted with radar. There should have been two radar boats, but someone had goofed in moving the second out, a line had fouled around its propeller, immobilizing it, and it would be a diver's job to get it loose. There was no time for that. The invasion went on with one radar boat. On the way inshore one of the three remaining guide boats had been sunk by enemy shellfire. Another boat had gone to its assistance, leaving one guide boat.

At Slapton Sands when smoke had been used by the "invaders" the smoke had blown back on them as they came in from the sea and confused their vision. So no smoke was used this day in the assault, but there was plenty of smoke from the barrage against the beaches and again there was an offshore breeze. So the skipper of the one remaining guide boat had been confused by the smoke and dust ashore. Further, no one had taken account of the tidal stream that flows at three knots southward into the Bay of the Seine on the flood. The result was a landing where it ought not to have been made.

What was to be done? The leading company commander arrived at the stone wall. He stopped. Brigadier General Theodore Roosevelt, Jr., the son of the former President, was in that assault wave. He was assistant division commander of the 4th Division. He stopped too, then went on, over the seawall to the top of a dune, and looked around. He saw the high dune line of les Dunes de Varreville and the windmill. They were a mile from their destination. He came back down to the beach.

The company officers were talking about moving west to the proper area, along the beach.

Fortunately, General Roosevelt had the presence of mind to stop that suicidal movement. During Operation Tiger, some troops had also landed in the wrong place and had moved across to the right area without regard for the reaction of the "enemy." The umpires had roasted them for this. After Operation Tiger, Admiral Moon and General Collins had warned that the men must be ready to improvise, and General Roosevelt was there to do it. There was no question now of taking their assigned targets. As Roosevelt knew, the really important matter was to get ashore, go inland and there to link up with the paratroop units to capture those causeways and the roads and towns beyond. There on the beach he organized the offense, and the two assault battalions moved up the two middle beach exits, advancing across the flooded area to Normandy proper and the hard ground. As the 1st Battalion crossed toward Audouville-la-Hubert, the 2nd Battalion turned south to go along the Pouppeville road. The surprise was almost complete, the opposition lighter than it would have been had they landed in the proper place. So much for plans, and so much more for brilliant innovation. General Roosevelt ultimately received the Medal of Honor for his work that day.

At H+45 the 1st Engineer Special Brigade began coming ashore on the new beach. Colonel Caffey was still in charge, General Bradley's complaints on the occasion of Exercise Tiger having been conveniently mislaid by the First Army staff when they learned the truth, that the engineers had been badly hit in the battle of the LSTs. (General Bradley learned nothing of the true reason for the problems of the engineers until the end of the war; then he was a little shamefaced about his remarks.)

The brigade and the naval demolition parties were supposed to clear the underwater obstacles. But the underwater obstacles in this area were virtually nonexistent and nary a man got his feet wet in clearing up the beach. There had been talk of blowing fifty-foot gaps in the defenses and bringing in the supplies thus. The umpires of Slapton Sands had made much of this. But, in fact, it had all turned out quite differently. There were not enough defenses to occasion any fifty-foot gaps, and the entire beach was cleared in less than an hour. There was that four-foot seawall behind the beach to be dealt with and the engineers blew holes in it sufficient for tanks and trucks to pass through. They also found minefields here and there and cleared them out. Then they began to work on the roads that would lead up to the beach exits of the causeway. They came under sporadic shelling, but the whole was as nothing compared to what they had been through before in Italy and what they had expected.

Soon road development was well along, and supplies were coming in to temporary dumps right in back of the beach. Still, they were not seeing any Germans.

By nine o'clock the American 4th Division troops had crossed the dunes, encountering a few Germans, and were running up against pillboxes on the other side. The amphibious tanks were coming ashore just then, and they were brought into action through the gaps in the seawall blown by the engineers.

Soon one advance party had reached Exit 1, the most southerly of the causeway exits. It led to Pouppeville and from there to Ste. Marie-du-Mont. In the middle of the causeway was a little bridge. As the Americans came up from the beach, a handful of Germans came running down the causeway, saw them, and ducked down underneath. The men of the 4th Division heard shooting from the Pouppeville direction and saw troops coming along the causeway from that side. They raised the orange flags they had been given for recognition if these were American parachutists, and the shooting stopped.

The Germans were still down there under the bridge, and they were caught between the two forces. After the Germans had been dealt with, the 4th Division troops met the 101st Airborne troops. It was not quite the right place, and the paratroops were not quite the right people—the plan for Normandy had called for them to meet the 82nd Airborne, as they had at Slapton Sands. But the principle was sound, just as it had been at Slapton Sands. The 4th Division had taken its objectives, done what had to be done, and had lost only 200 men, far fewer than were killed in the battle of the LSTs.

After the fact the British marveled at the "good luck" of Force U. The other American landing at Omaha Beach had been much more difficult and much more costly in lives. The Germans, supposed to have only a second-rate regiment along the Atlantic Wall at this point, had quietly reinforced it with a regiment of first-rate troops, and the Allied intelligence apparatus had failed to pick up the change. No plan from Slapton Sands could have controlled this problem. V Corps had suffered 2,000 casualties on D-Day. The British casualties had also been high.

But by taking advantage of a difficulty, and bringing victory out of confusion, General Roosevelt had brought the leading elements of the 4th Division ashore with about twenty-five men killed and a hundred wounded in the initial assault. Luck? Of course there was luck, and the good sense to exploit it. For there were plenty of Germans around as the Allies discovered in the next few days. As the Germans began to pull themselves together in the Cotentin Peninsula, the 4th Division's casualties began to mount.

Even so, the "luck" of the Allies held. Concurrent to the assault on Normandy came loud noises from England indicating a new and even greater attack on the Pas de Calais, delivered by radio, double agents' spy reports, air strike, and every other means at the Allied disposal. The Germans believed. Field Marshal von Rundstedt maintained the strength of the 15th Army in the east. Rommel fought with the forces at hand, augmented by what he could get from Hitler. For a solid month the Germans hesitated to throw all their forces into the Normandy battle, and by the time they realized they had been gulled, it was too late. Operation Deception had been an enormous success and certainly contributed very heavily to the victory of the Allies in France.

Thus was vindicated the overwhelming concern of SHAEF with security, which had led to the concealment of the tragedy at Slapton Sands on April 28. To some, notably such peripheral participants as the medics at the hospitals that treated the casualties of the LST battle, the attitude of the SHAEF authorities and the security men seemed brutal and authoritarian. The wounded and their caretakers were threatened, no doubt about it. The experience left scars that lasted for years. After the war, men who had been there continued to grumble that Operation Tiger had been one of the great foul-ups of the Allies and that those hundreds of men had been sacrificed needlessly. Some soldiers even believed that the casualties had been concealed in the total casualties for the Normandy invasion.

But the fact is that the army did not forget Slapton Sands. When time had passed, and the invasion was long finished, the great grave was opened, the bodies were removed and properly buried. Some of the victims of the E-boat attack were buried in other cemeteries. A plaque was finally erected to remind the world and to thank the English for their assistance. Still the "secret" remained, and rumors were passed from time to time, culminating in the spate of rumors in early 1984 that pointed to dark doings by high authority at Slapton Sands.

Certainly, the tragedy of the LSTs was heightened by errors. Whether or not they could have been avoided is another matter. Given the frenetic pace of Allied preparations on the eve of the invasion of France, it is not so remarkable that errors were made, as that so few errors were made and so few lives lost in what some regarded as a "useless" manner.

But the fact is that Operation Tiger was not "useless," and that the deaths of those soldiers and sailors aboard the LSTs were not meaningless. Many lessons were learned by high officialdom at Slapton Sands, and the deaths of those men put a stamp of authority on the corrective measures that was not forgotten by the people involved.

Operation Tiger was neither a total foul-up nor a waste of time. Given the circumstances that prevailed, the tragedy probably could not have been avoided. The men who died there in Lyme Bay on that chilly April morning contributed very heavily to the success of the landings that were carried out in France just six weeks later.

Prelude to Victory, one might call Operation Tiger.

Acknowledgments

I AM indebted to a number of people who helped me in the preparation of this book. Dr. Ralph C. Greene, of Chicago, wrote me regarding the subject; he has been amassing material for a number of years, since he was a medical officer in one of the hospitals where casualties of Operation Tiger were taken. Soon he should be publishing an account of his own.

Barnett Hoffner of Brooklyn, New York, was enormously helpful to me in this undertaking. He was a sergeant of engineers and was on the beach at Slapton Sands.

Colonel James K. Gaynor was also extremely helpful. He was the designer of the training area at Slapton Sands in 1943-44.

Lieutenant Colonel Robert T. Frank, of the Center of Military History, steered me to sources.

Dr. Dean Allard and the staff of the Navy Historical Center at the Washington Navy Yard extended themselves as they always do to help researchers. I am also grateful to librarians at the Navy Library in the Navy Yard for assistance.

Richard J. Sommers, Archivist-Historian of the Army Military History Institute found for me several documents relative to Operation Tiger as did David A. Keough. John J. Slonaker, chief of the Historical Reference Branch of the Institute also found materials.

Dr. Gibson B. Smith of the modern military branch of the U.S. National Archives spent many hours on the SHAEF files in my behalf.

I am indebted to Diana Hoyt for other research materials and to Olga G. Hoyt for her always faithful assistance in a dozen different ways from research and typing to editing.

Notes

Introduction

The *New York Times* article by Jon Nordheimer appeared in the *Times* on April 25, 1984.

1

Planning

The quotations from Winston Churchill come from Volume III of his history, *The Second World War.* The material about General Morgan's appointment and early problems is from his own *Overture to Overlord.* The material about Operation Starkey is from the Morgan book, from Jock Haswell's *D-Day,* and from the files of SHAEF.

2

Enter Eisenhower

David Howarth's *D-Day,* chapter one, contains an excellent summary of the career of General Eisenhower prior to his assumption of command of SHAEF. That was what I used. The story of the Marshall–Churchill discussions and visits is from Churchill. The story of the bickering between the United States and Britain is from Churchill, Howarth, Bradley, and Eisenhower. General Morgan's visit to Washington is from his own book. The tale of Eisenhower's "friend," the critical Briton, is from Captain Butcher's memoir, as is the report on AP Correspondent Wes Gallagher's observations. The reprise of Hitler's defense order for the west is from an unpublished manuscript of my own, *Hitler's War.* So is the study of Hitler's reasoning and motivation. The notes about von Rundstedt and Rommel are from Hans Speidel's *Invasion 1944.* The notes about Eisenhower's reaction to the plan for Operation Overlord are from Butcher and Montgomery.

3

Preparations for Invasion

Notes on the establishment of the Assault Training Center are from the files of SHAEF. The account of the SHAEF meeting of January 23, 1944, is contained in a minute of the meeting. The reports of changes in planning are from Butcher, Eisenhower, Montgomery, Morgan, and Bradley's accounts. The discussion of corps commanders is from Bradley's account. So is the discussion of Bradley's argument with Air Chief Marshal Leigh-Mallory about the airborne landings. The material about the Mulberries comes from several books on the Mulberry operation and from Morgan. The story of the Allied leaders playing with boats in a bathtub comes from Hartcup's *Code Name Mulberry.*

The note about Eisenhower's troops inspections comes from his correspondence with General Marshall in the spring of 1944. (Eisenhower library.)

The material about the Allied troop movement within England is from Bradley, Butcher, and the plan for Operation Tiger.

4

Putting it All Together

The discussion of the difficulties of assembling Allied armies with different customs, logistical situations, and arms is from Morgan, primarily. The discussion of transport difficulties is from Bykovsky and Larson's *The Transportation Corps, Operations Overseas,* a part of the *U.S. Army History of World War II.* The problems of the navy and landing craft are from various accounts, and the files of SHAEF. The matter of American armor and its deficiencies is discussed in several works, including Bradley's; and particularly in General James M. Gavin's memoirs, *On to Berlin.* Von Rundstedt's appraisal is from Speidel. The peat-on-the-beaches story is from Morgan. The training program is discussed in Morgan and in Bradley, and the SHAEF records have several mentions of various aspects.

5

Security

The Eisenhower statement about security is contained in a letter of July 30, 1948, to Major General E. B. Lyon of the U.S. Air Force regarding General Miller's case. The material about Bigot procedure is from a SHAEF report on the subject by Colonel Charles C. Blakeney. The Chicago "espionage" tale comes from several sources; Morgan, Haswell are the best.

The note from Prime Minister Churchill to General Eisenhower about the "prominent military writer" is from the SHAEF files. The Eisenhower directive is also from the SHAEF files.

The Miller case is thoroughly discussed in General Eisenhower's correspondence with General Marshall of April 1944. General Sibert's letter to General Bradley is from the Eisenhower library. So is the Canadian businessman's letter. The discussion of limitation of travel and diplomatic correspondence is from Morgan and from correspondence between Eisenhower and Prime Minister Churchill in the SHAEF files. The McCormick story is from a memo in the SHAEF files.

6

Operation Deception

Morgan was the source of much of this chapter, as was Haswell. David Kahn's *Hitler's Spies* was also valuable. The material about the Mulberries is from Morgan and the several Mulberry books. Farago and Kahn contributed to the discussions of the Allied deception, as did the book on Ultra and *The Wizard War.* The story of the Enigma machine is from *Ultra in the West* and from *MI5.* The material about the Atlantic Wall is from Speidel and my own unpublished history of Hitler's war. Operation Bodyguard is discussed by Morgan and by Kahn and Haswell. The story of Hubert is from Kahn. Also the tales of Brutus and Tramp. The story of Patton's First Army Group is from Morgan, Bradley, and Haswell.

7

Operation Tiger

The material about Admiral Leatham and the Devonport command is from the naval reports on Operation Tiger, all of which have been compiled in the U.S. Navy Historical Center at the Washington Navy Yard on a single 35 mm film. The material about the various training operations is from a report of the 1st Engineers Special Brigade in the files of the Army Historical Center at Carlisle Barracks. The material about the plan of Operation Tiger is from the plans as put forth by VII Corps, and the corps war diary.

The note about the Stettinius visit is from a press release in the files of VII Corps at Suitland. The notes about the tides come from Bradley's book and from Morgan. The fictitious situation report on the Devon coast is from the VII Corps plan for Operation Tiger. The reports on planning and pre-exercise matters are from the VII Corps report file. The naval reports are from Admiral Moon's action report, and from various war diaries.

8

Attack!

The story of Operation Tiger comes from the VII Corps war diary, the Naval task force war diary, and the files of SHAEF relative to the operations. Some notes are from the observations of General Bradley and Captain Butcher. The notes about the 6th Engineers Special Brigade are from a letter to the author from Barnett Hoffner. The notes about engineer performance on the beaches are largely from the umpires' reports on Exercise Tiger, in the VII Corps papers. The tale about General Huebner is from Hoffner.

9

The E-Boat Attack

The material about the LST convoy is from the naval records, the various

LST action reports, and the action reports of Admiral Moon and others, and interviews with various British officers who were involved, all in the Navy Historical Center files in Washington.

10

After the Attack

The material about the Allied naval forces is all from the action reports and statements of Allied officers at the time.

11

Assessment

The various assessments, 4th Division, 101st Airborne, Umpires, VII Corps, 1st Army, are all in the files of the VII Corps and of SHAEF. The engineers made their own assessment, which is in the papers at the Carlisle Barracks. The quotations from General Bradley are from his own book.

12

Remedies

Various remedies were proposed by various officers in action reports. Most of the suggestions were taken seriously and some, acted upon, brought considerable savings in time and perhaps in lives later on.

13

General Collins's Findings

This section of the book dwells heavily on the report and critique of Operation Tiger held by General Collins after the end of the exercise. All concerned commanders were invited and urged to speak up. It was not a matter of trying to place blame for errors, General Collins assured them at the beginning of the session, but a matter of finding out what various things went wrong so they could be corrected before June 5, the day planned for the invasion of France. This reassurance indeed brought the officers to speak frankly, and out of the critique came a number of useful changes. Only the engineers seemed to feel that the exercises and the critiques were a waste of time, and from their point of view, that was probably true. No exercise could possibly duplicate the actuality for engineers, who would be under fire on the open beaches, most of the time.

14

Where Are the Bigots?

How close the losses in Operation Tiger came to stopping the buildup for the invasion of France will never be known, but there were strong elements within the British camp that wanted to stop the invasion, even at this late date and they made much of the loss. Consequently, General Montgomery conducted a thorough investigation. What put an end to speculation was the finding of the bodies of all the engineer officers of the 1st Engineers Special Brigade who could possibly have had any of the major secrets of the invasion. Several other officers bodies were not found, but these were company officers who had not been made party to any Bigot secrets. But for a time, as Major Ingersoll indicated in his book *Top Secret,* a large flap was brewing at Montgomery's headquarters. Ingersoll contributed to it with the announcement that there had been plenty of chance for the Germans to have taken prisoners even though the Admiralty explanation of the affair indicated not. So the 231st Army Group went charging off in several directions and was not satisfied until all those bodies were found.

The account of the Fabius operations is from the 1st Engineer Special Brigade's report.

15

Month of Trials

The month just before D-Day was nervewracking for all concerned. The Allies counted the days and watched as the Germans made changes in their defenses. The weather created enormous problems. So did changes in the German espionage system and some unfortunate captures of partisans on the far side of the channel. The troops were cooped up and becoming restless. There were more security problems, and they seemed more important as the invasion neared. Two thousand security men surrounded the American troops in their "sausages," and they were very stiff with anyone who even looked as though he might want to go over the wire. At SHAEF there was a sudden panic over the condition of the artificial harbors, for it seemed they would never be ready on time. But the British muddled through as they were wont to do, all was finally put together, and even the weather ultimately cooperated for a few hours.

16

The Proof of the Pudding

Perhaps Air Chief Marshall Leigh-Mallory had been right. If the American air drop had gone as it ought to have, perhaps the American airborne troops would have been slaughtered as they landed. But the airdrop went so badly that it proved a blessing; the Germans were thoroughly confused because so many units dropped in so many areas, and they never did mount a satisfactory attack against the beachhead area in the first twenty-four hours of action. In addition, small units of the airborne managed to carry out the major aims of the two divisions, so all went well, and in the end Air Chief Marshal Leigh-Mallory apologized to Eisenhower in one of those handsome gestures of which the British are capable. The stories of what happened on the beaches and behind them are from various accounts of the first hours of the invasion, including a number of letters and accounts I have collected for a yet unpublished book on the American war effort in Europe.

17

The Lessons Learned

This chapter depended on the various reports of Operation Tiger, as compared with the realities of the invasion. It is not hard after comparing them to see the lessons learned and to realize that Operation Tiger was indeed successful beyond the dreams of its planners, because, if nothing else, it convinced all involved that they had to be "flexible" and ready for the unexpected. General Roosevelt certainly made an asset of error. The troops were landed a mile away from their destination. Roosevelt might have elected to try to get to the proper beach, and the Germans might have sliced them down on the way; at least, the enemy would have been well warned. But when Roosevelt saw that the troops had been landed in the wrong place, he decided that his beach should be the major invasion beach. By bringing everything there, the Americans were able to strike straight up across the beaches and the flooded territory to the French mainland, and the surprise of the enemy was complete, and the American casualties were minimal. If there were a thousand casualties and more than 800 dead in Operation Tiger, the handful of casualties at Utah Beach on D-Day certainly made up for it.

Bibliography

Published Materials

Belfield, Eversley, and H. Essame. *The Battle for Normandy.* Philadelphia: Dufour Editions, 1965.

Bennett, Ralph. *Ultra in the West.* New York: Scribners, 1979.

Churchill, Winston. *The Second World War.* 6 vols. Boston: Houghton Mifflin, 1948–53.

Edwards, Kenneth Commander. *Operation Neptune.* London: Collins, 1946.

Bradley, Omar N. *A Soldier's Story.* New York: Henry Holt and Co., 1951.

Butcher, Harry C. *My Three Years With Eisenhower.* New York: Simon and Schuster, 1946.

Eisenhower, Dwight D. *Crusade In Europe.* New York: Doubleday and Co., 1948.

Farago, Ladislas. *The Game of the Foxes.* New York: David McKay, 1971.

Harrison, Gordon A. *Cross Channel Attack.* Washington: Department of the Army, 1951.

Hartcup, Guy. *Code Name Mulberry.* Newton Abbot, Devon, England: David & Charles, 1977.

Haswell, Jock. *D-Day.* New York: Times Books, 1979.

Howarth, David. *D-Day.* New York: McGraw Hill, 1959.

Ingersoll, Ralph. *Top Secret.* New York: Harcourt Brace, 1946.

Jones, R. V. *The Wizard War.* New York: Coward McCann & Geoghegen, 1978.

Kahn, David. *Hitler's Spies.* New York: Macmillan, 1978.

Montgomery, Field Marshal The Viscount of Alamein, K.G., G.C.B., D.S.O. *Normandy to the Baltic.* London: Hutchinson, 1947.

Morgan, Sir Frederick, K.C.B. *Overture to Overlord.* New York: Doubleday, 1950.

Paine, Lauren. *D-Day.* London: Robert Hale, 1981.

Speidel, Hans. *Invasion 1944.* Chicago: Henry Regnery Co., 1950.

Taylor, Maxwell D. *Swords and Plowshares.* New York: W. W. Norton, 1972.

Turner, John Frayn. *Invasion.* London: George G. Harrap & Co., Ltd., 1959.

Warner, Philip. *The D Day Landings.* London: William Kimber, 1980.

Weigley, Russell F. *Eisenhower's Lieutenants.* Bloomington: Indiana University Press, 1981.

West, Nigel. *MI 5.* New York: Stein and Day, 1982.

Unpublished Materials

From the U.S. National Archives, Suitland, Md.

Summary, Exercise Tiger, Hqs VII Corps U.S. Army.

Summary, Exercise Tiger, First U.S. Army.

Comments, Exercise Tiger, Headquarters First United States Army.

History, 1st Engineer Special Brigade.

Report of Enemy Action (LST battle), Headquarters Sub Area V.

Operation Tiger, S-3 Periodic Report, 27 April 1944.

Operation Tiger, G-3 Journal VII Corps, 28 April 1944.

Report on Participation of 101st Airborne Division in Exercise Tiger, VII Corps.

Exercise Tiger VII Corps Umpires report.

VII Corps Report on Air Missions for Exercise Tiger.

4th Division Orders for Exercise Tiger.

Minutes of First Army reprise of Operation Tiger.

SHAEF Records, U.S. National Archives, Washington, D.C.

Messages, April–May 1944.

Minutes of Meetings of COSSAC staff, 1943–44.

Report on Bigot Procedure, COSSAC G-2, November 19, 1943.

War Cabinet report to Chiefs of Staff on Overlord, 1 June, 1944.

War Cabinet Chiefs of Staff Committee report on Appledore Combined Training Area, 21 July 1943.

Meeting to Discuss Revision of Agenda for course at Largs, 28 June 1943.

Draft Letter, General Eisenhower to Prime Minister Churchill regarding communications bans, undated (obviously May 1944).

SHAEF reports, Exercise Tiger, April–May 1944.

COSSAC report on Supply of Landing Craft for Operation Overlord, 30 September 1943.

Minutes of meeting convened by Supreme Commander, Norfolk House, 21 January 1944.

SHAEF Memorandum on Intelligence function, 28 August 1943.

Dwight D. Eisenhower Library, Abilene, Kansas.

Exchange of correspondence DDE and Major General Henry Miller, 1944.

Correspondence of General Eisenhower relative to Major General Henry Miller, 1944, 1945, 1948.

Correspondence of General Eisenhower relative to security matters, 1944.

MS notes of Captain Harry Butcher re Operation Tiger.

Letter DDE to General Marshall re General Patton and security generally.

Memo 19 April 1944, General E. L. Sibert, accusing General Miller of drunkenness and loose talk.

Department of the Army
U.S. Army Military History Institute
Carlisle Barracks, Pennsylvania

Forgy papers, including list of 1st Engineer Special Brigade casualties in Operation Tiger.

The Other D-Days: Report on Operation Tiger.

Passing in Review: Story of American Graves Registration Command in Europe and Africa by Colonel L. R. Talbot.

Index